The Salem Witch Trials

by Earle Rice Jr.

Lucent Books, San Diego, CA

Other books in the Famous Trials series:

The Dred Scott Decision
The Nuremberg Trials
The O.J. Simpson Trial
The Scopes Trial
The Trial of Socrates

Library of Congress Cataloging-in-Publication Data

Rice, Earle.
    The Salem witch trials / by Earle Rice Jr.
      p. cm. — (Famous trials)
    Includes bibliographical references and index.
    Summary: Discusses the historical setting of the witchcraft trials in colonial Salem, Massachusetts, with background information on the Puritans.
    ISBN 1-56006-272-X (alk. paper)
    1.Witchcraft—Massachusetts—Salem—History—Juvenile literature. 2. Trials (Witchcraft)—Massachusetts—Salem—Juvenile literature. 3. Salem (Mass.)—History—Juvenile literature. 4. Salem (Mass.)—Social conditions—Juvenile literature. [1. Witchcraft—Massachusetts—Salem. 2. Trials (Witchcraft)—Massachusetts—Salem. 3. Salem (Mass.)—History—Colonial period, ca. 1600-1775.]
I. Title. II. Series: Famous trials series.
BF1575.R53 1997
133.4'3'097445—dc20   96-31425
                                     CIP
                                     AC

Copyright © 1997 by Lucent Books, Inc.
P.O. Box 289011
San Diego, CA 92198-9011
Printed in the U.S.A.

Table of Contents

Foreword

"The law is not an end in and of itself, nor does it provide ends. It is preeminently a means to serve what we think is right."

William J. Brennan Jr.

THE CONCEPT OF JUSTICE AND THE RULE OF LAW are hallmarks of Western civilization, manifested perhaps most visibly in widely famous and dramatic court trials. These trials include such important and memorable personages as the ancient Greek philosopher Socrates, who was accused and convicted of corrupting the minds of his society's youth in 399 B.C.; the French maiden and military leader Joan of Arc, accused and convicted of heresy against the church in 1431; and former football star O. J. Simpson, acquitted of double murder in 1995. These and other well-known and controversial trials constitute the most public, and therefore most familiar, demonstrations of a Western legal tradition that dates back through the ages. Although no one is certain when the first law code appeared or when the first formal court trials were held, Babylonian ruler Hammurabi introduced the first known law code in about 1760 B.C. It remains unclear how this code was administered, and no records of specific trials have survived. What is clear, however, is that humans have always sought to govern behavior and define actions in terms of law.

Almost all societies have made laws and prosecuted people for going against those laws, but the question of which behaviors to sanction and which to censure has always been controversial and remains in flux. Some, such as Roman orator and legislator Cicero, argue that laws are simply applications of universal standards. Cicero believed that humanity would agree on what constituted illegal behavior and that human laws were a mere extension of natural laws. "True law is right reason in agreement with nature," he wrote,

4

world-wide in scope, unchanging, everlasting. . . . We may not oppose or alter that law, we cannot abolish it, we cannot be freed from its obligations by any legislature. . . . This [natural] law does not differ for Rome and for Athens, for the present and for the future. . . . It is and will be valid for all nations and all times.

Cicero's rather optimistic view has been contradicted throughout history, however. For every law made to preserve harmony and set universal standards of behavior, another has been born of fear, prejudice, greed, desire for power, and a host of other motives. History is replete with individuals defying and fighting to change such laws—and even to topple governments that dictate such laws. Abolitionists fought against slavery, civil rights leaders fought for equal rights, millions throughout the world have fought for independence—these constitute a minimum of reasons for which people have sought to overturn laws that they believed to be wrong or unjust. In opposition to Cicero, then, many others, such as eighteenth-century English poet and philosopher William Godwin, believe humans must be constantly vigilant against bad laws. As Godwin said in 1793:

Laws we sometimes call the wisdom of our ancestors. But this is a strange imposition. It was as frequently the dictate of their passion, of timidity, jealousy, a monopolizing spirit, and a lust of power that knew no bounds. Are we not obliged perpetually to renew and remodel this misnamed wisdom of our ancestors? To correct it by a detection of their ignorance, and a censure of their intolerance?

Lucent Books' *Famous Trials* series showcases trials that exemplify both society's praiseworthy condemnation of universally unacceptable behavior and its misguided persecution of individuals based on fear and ignorance, as well as trials that leave open the question of whether justice has been done. Each volume begins by setting the scene and providing a historical context to show how society's mores influence the trial process and the verdict. Each book goes on to present a detailed and lively account of the trial, including liberal use of primary source material such as direct testimony, lawyers' summations, and contemporary and modern commentary. In addition, sidebars throughout the text create a broader context by presenting illuminating details about important points of law, information on key personalities, and important distinctions related to civil, federal, and criminal procedures. Thus, all of the primary and secondary source material included in both the text and the sidebars demonstrates to readers the sources and methods historians use to derive information and conclusions about such events.

Lastly, each *Famous Trials* volume includes one or more of the following comprehensive tools that motivate readers to pursue further reading and research. A timeline allows readers to see the scope of the trial at a glance, annotated bibliographies provide both sources for further research and a thorough list of works consulted, a glossary helps students with unfamiliar words and concepts, and a comprehensive index permits quick scanning of the book as a whole.

The insight of Oliver Wendell Holmes Jr., distinguished Supreme Court justice, exemplifies the theme of the *Famous Trials* series. Taken from *The Common Law*, published in 1881, Holmes remarked: "The life of the law has not been logic, it has been experience." That "experience" consists mainly in how laws are applied in society and challenged in the courts, a process resulting in differing outcomes from one generation to the next. Thus, the *Famous Trials* series encourages readers to examine trials within a broader historical and social context.

Introduction

The Puritan Way

*T*HE DEVIL'S WORK IN SALEM VILLAGE *began during a chill autumn evening in November 1691. Ironically, it began in the parsonage of a Puritan minister devoted to the Lord's work. Unknown to the minister, a few young Puritan girls—including his nine-year-old daughter, Elizabeth—had started to gather at night in his rectory while he was visiting with parish members. The impressionable young girls hoped to learn of their futures through the occult powers of the minister's mysterious household servant Tituba.*

Following a failed business venture in Barbados, the minister had returned to the Massachusetts Bay Colony two years earlier, bringing with him a wife, three children, a niece, and Tituba and John Indian, a Carib Indian couple. When the work of his calling occupied the minister, and his wife was ailing or away visiting, he entrusted the care of his daughter Elizabeth and his eleven-year-old niece, Abigail Williams, to the slave Tituba.

On that still and frosty evening, Tituba entertained the girls by firelight, spinning tales of witchcraft and black magic. Flickering flames from the fire cast eerie dancing shadows on the walls. Captivated by the Carib storyteller, Betty, as the youngest girl was called, and Abigail listened with rapt attention. Their eyes widened with anticipation when Tituba dropped an egg white into a glass of water to create a makeshift crystal ball. Seeking glimpses of romance and fortune—whom they will marry, what his calling will be, whether they will be rich—the girls peered through the murky glass and into the future.

The egg white settled slowly to the bottom of the glass. Suddenly one of the girls—probably Betty—gasped. Instead of a romantic vision of things to come, she saw the ominous form of a coffin beginning to take shape in the milky whiteness. Whether the product of witchery or black magic or the yield of a child's fertile imagination, the spectral image of the coffin foretold of the evil craze so soon to seize and possess Salem Village.

Witches and Witchcraft

Witches and witchcraft, of course, did not originate with the Puritans in seventeenth-century New England. Witches, usually credited with malevolent supernatural powers, and witchery date back to pagan times. Numerous mentions of witches appear in the Bible, notably "the witch of Endor" (although not so worded in the Bible), a woman who had a "familiar spirit" through whom Saul sought to communicate with the dead Samuel. (A *familiar* or *familiar spirit* is a spirit slave, sometimes embodied in human shape, sometimes appearing as a cat, dog, raven, or other animal. It serves a witch, wizard, or sorcerer and is thought to be a demon in disguise.) According to the Bible (1 Samuel 28:7), this woman brought Samuel up "out of the earth" after Saul promised not to take action against her as a witch.

England and Scotland declared witchcraft a felony in 1542 and instituted the death penalty in 1563 against anyone causing death by witchery. Such law enactments inspired a century of witch-hunts in then Presbyterian-controlled England. These witch-hunts continued as a favorite Presbyterian pastime until the Restoration (in British history, the return of the Stuarts to the throne in 1660, in the person of Charles II, thus bringing the Puritan Commonwealth to an end). It was during this frantic, witch-hating atmosphere that the first Puritans sailed for the New World.

King James I of England persecuted the Puritans, driving many of them out of England and to the American colonies.

Women accused of witchcraft are hanged in a public square in Europe.

A New and Hopeful World

The Puritans—members of a sixteenth- and seventeenth-century Protestant group in England and New England—opposed certain religious practices and ceremonies of the state Church of England derived from the Roman Catholic Church. Favoring simplicity of worship, the Puritans spoke out against written prayers, religious icons and pictures in churches, instrumental music at services, and so on. Their appeal to King James I of England to "purify" the state church and rid it of Catholic procedures drew the king's wrath. "I will make them conform or I will harry them out of the land," vowed the irate James. King James I and his successor, Charles I, followed through on James's threat of harassment, resulting in the exodus of thousands of Puritans to the New World in the 1600s.

A band of Puritans called Separatists migrated first to Holland in 1608, then on to America in 1620, where they founded Plymouth Colony. A decade later, after obtaining a charter from

Puritans push off European shores to board a ship that will take them to the American colonies and—they hoped—religious freedom.

the English Crown, another band of Puritans sailed for New England and established the Massachusetts Bay Colony.

The Puritans came to America with dreams of fashioning a new and better life in a new and hopeful world, a world free from religious persecution. But along with new hope and a spartan faith, they brought with them a parcel of old superstitions and a medieval concept of women's place in their Lord's scheme of things entire. To better understand how the Puritan colonists so readily accepted and feared the existence of witches and other agents of the devil, it helps to examine the misconceptions of their age. Only a superficial inquiry into Puritan beliefs, attitudes, and ways is needed to realize how the consequent lifestyle so facilely produced a spawning ground for Salem's scourge of witchery.

Puritan Life

In founding a new colony in Massachusetts, the Puritans believed that they were entering into a sacred compact with God, agreeing to live in accordance with his will in return for a divine mandate in the new world. They arrived in America intent on establishing God's kingdom on earth. It became the duty of each individual to keep faith with the collective covenant with God. To commune with Satan, the lord of evil, or to inscribe one's name in his book (a book signed by witches to enlist in the service of the devil), invited God's wrath and exposed the entire community to the threat of divine retribution. In this context, individual sin exceeded mere personal failing; individual sin constituted an act of treason.

The Puritans viewed the world in basic black and white, with the forces of evil engaged in an unceasing battle for the souls of the Lord's legions. Their towns and villages stood as bastions of righteousness surrounded by armies of dark intent in the form of devil worshipers, hostile Indians, and the ravages of nature. Discipline and devotion became their watchwords in the service of the Lord. Puritan New England, as described by historian Sally Smith Booth, was a place where

> almost every aspect of an individual's life was closely regulated by church dogma. . . . Games, dancing, social gatherings, and physical recreation were all forbidden as evil practices. Repression of sexual activities . . . was stringent and open display of affection was frowned upon.

The simplest acts of innocence—talking to a pet or calling it by name, joining children in play, humming, singing, or otherwise making music, daydreaming, hiking in the woods—might be looked upon as peculiar, even questionable, conduct.

The Puritans embraced the European heritage of subjugating women to the will and wants of men. Simply stated, the Puritans were misogynists—a five-dollar term for woman haters. Also, the fit among the Puritans looked with a jaundiced eye upon the unfit. The ill, the crippled, the poor, and the old were treated with disdain. Those born with crippling defects, for example, were thought to be offspring of the devil. Impoverished women too old to bear children became overtly unwanted burdens on Puritan society. Even the most superficial look at the

THE FIRST WITCH TRIAL

The Massachusetts Bay Colony conducted its first witch trial in 1648, almost a half century before the infamous Salem witch trials. Margaret Jones, a Charlestown midwife and lay healer, became the person to be tried in the colony as a witch. Writers of that time who witnessed her trial and its aftermath failed to describe either Margaret as a person or the details of the event. But Governor John Winthrop kept a journal outlining the accusations against her. His writings constituted an overview of all known English witch lore to date and established precedents for future use in Salem:

> The evidence against her was, (1) that she was found to have a malignant touch as many persons (men, women, and children) who she stroked or touched with any affection or displeasure, or, etc., were taken with deafness, or vomiting, or other violent pains or sickness; (2) she practicing physic, and her medicines being such things as (by her own confession) as were harmless, as aniseed, liquors, etc., yet had extraordinary violent effects; (3) she would use to tell such as would not make use of her physic that they would never be healed, and accordingly their diseases and hurts continued, with relapse against the ordinary course, and beyond the apprehension of all physicians and surgeons; (4) some things which she foretold came to pass accordingly; other things she could tell of (as secret speeches, etc.) which she had not ordinary means to come to the knowledge of; (5) she had (upon search) an apparent teat [witch's teat] in her secret parts as fresh as if it had been newly sucked and after it had been scanned, upon a forced search, that was withered, and another began on the opposite side; (6) in the prison, in the clear daylight, there was seen in her arms, sitting on the floor, and her clothes up, etc., a little child, which ran from her into another room, and the officer following it, it was vanished. The like child was seen in two other places, to which she had relation; and one maid that saw it, fell sick upon it, and was cured by the said Margaret, who used means to be employed to that end. Her behavior at her trial was very intemperate, lying notoriously, and railing upon the jury and witnesses, etc., and in the like distemper she died. The same day and hour she was executed, there was a very great tempest at Connecticut, which blew down many trees, etc.

John Hale, a pastor from Beverly, noted that one of Jones's neighbors testified that he had "prayed her to consider if God did not bring this punishment upon her for some other crime, and asked, if she had not been guilty of stealing many years ago." The writings of Hale and his contemporaries indicate that stealing was one of several crimes—such as promiscuity and infanticide—generally associated with witchcraft. Margaret Jones confessed to stealing and was hanged as a witch.

Puritans, exiled from their community, are forced to try and make a life on their own. Puritans considered exile worse than a death sentence.

Puritan way reveals a culture stained by ignorance and hypocrisy; a culture in which men dominated women and the strong ruled the weak; a culture in turmoil, struggling to survive failed crops and hostile Indians. These are but a few of the facets of the Puritan way that led to tragedy in an age and place primed for still another witch-hunt.

Chapter 1

Tituba's Circle

L IFE WAS HARD IN THE OLD BAY COLONY of Massachusetts. By
1691 the Puritans had been forced to endure smallpox epi-
demics, Indian raids, and the loss of self-rule that they enjoyed
under the terms of the original Massachusetts charter issued by
Charles I of England. The English Crown had revoked the colonial charter in 1684 and had subsequently appointed Sir Edmund
Andros as the colony's first royal governor in 1686.

Andros promptly informed the colonists that all land titles
granted under the revoked charter were henceforth invalidated.
Three years later, heartened by the Glorious Revolution in

England in 1688, when
William and Mary replaced
James II on the throne, the
angered colonists over-
threw the hated Andros and
restored the old charter
government in 1689. This
minor revolt against the
Crown, as the colonists well
knew, would not end their
problems.

*Royal governor of the
Massachusetts colony, Sir
Edmund Andros was despised by
the colonists.*

For the next three years, the once vital, self-governing commonwealth drifted aimlessly in a sea of legal uncertainties. Community elders suffered fierce anxieties while they waited to learn what would happen to their land—acres cleared and tilled by generations of backbreaking toil—if the charter were permanently lost. Of equal concern to the Puritans was the potential loss of their freeperson status and the consequence of returning to some form of servitude.

Increase Mather, father of Cotton Mather, sailed to England to negotiate for colonists' rights.

The colonists' best hope for the legitimate restoration of their charter lay with the Reverend Increase Mather—father of Cotton Mather and minister of Boston's North Church. Increase had sailed for England in 1688 to negotiate with the Crown for a new charter. As 1691 drew to a close, rumors whispered throughout the colony held that God had frowned on Mather's negotiations and that he was giving up. For the God-fearing people of Massachusetts, it was not the best of times. And the worst lay just ahead.

Girls as young as Betty Parris and Abigail Williams, the daughter and niece, respectively, of the Reverend Parris, could scarcely be expected to fully grasp the uncertainties of their situation. But they most surely could sense the anxiety of their elders, induced by the hardships and uncertainties of their unsettled times, which in many adults was manifested by irascible behavior. For the younger girls of Salem Village, held virtually captive indoors by the wintry elements, the winter of 1691–92 became truly one of deepening discontent.

Winter in New England

If a Puritan girl were to have been asked in 1691 to choose one word to describe winters in New England, she might well have answered "boring." To the young, unspoken-for girls of Salem Village—housebound by sheets of icy wind and blankets of crusted snow—the drab winter days seemed to drag on in endless continuums of enforced monotony.

Conversely, men and boys happily greeted winter as a frosty respite from their labors in the fields. Their untillable frozen acres afforded them time to foray into nearby woods with muskets primed in ardent pursuit of wild turkey, deer, and an occasional marauding fox or wolf. Or they might snatch up a line and hook, cut through the ice of a neighboring pond, and delight in the joys of fishing. And when the hunters and fishermen returned from forest or pond, innumerable home maintenance and repair chores awaited their attention. Ennui, even in the clutch of winter's frigid grasp, was not a male affliction.

Nor did boredom distress the elder women of Salem Village, who went diligently about their year-round indoor tasks without regard to the wintry conditions outside. Admittedly, however, they missed some of summertime's pleasant diversions, such as berry-picking excursions, and carting food and drink to the men working

New England Puritans wend their way to church during the winter.

A typical New England pioneer's cabin indicates a spartan lifestyle. While the New England winters brought a brief respite from work for the men, women continued in their duties. Here, a woman spins wool, cooks a meal, and tends her baby while her husband looks on.

in the fields. For Salem's matrons and dowagers, hard work—however repetitious—served as a deterrent to even the worst cases of ennui. Such was not the case with Salem's younger girls.

Relegated to help with the ongoing domestic tasks—sewing, spinning, cooking, washing, and cleaning—the unattached girls, unlike their elders, were not hardened—or at least resigned—to the monotony of Puritan domesticity. Even occasional diversions necessitated by having to produce virtually everything they used or consumed—making bread, butter, cheese, beer, cider, clothes, candles, and so on—offered scant relief from the inescapable humdrum of their lot. To the teenage and younger girls of Salem Village, winter represented month upon month of close confinement and unremitting drudgery. Winter, in a word, was *boring*.

In the winter of 1691–92, Salem's ingenues sought to banish their boredom by entertaining Satan in a house dedicated to the Lord. Their explorations into occult phenomena grew out of a guileless, youthful curiosity. But their pursuit of unknown fantasies soon led the girls down a path lined with lies and deceit as they struggled to keep their furtive activities secret from their elders. And their forbidden flirtations with the devil unleashed what is perhaps the most famous witch-hunt of all time. Before their probings into Satan's dark domain ended, nineteen innocent Salemites were hanged on Gallows Hill, and another blameless soul was pressed to death by stones. The tragedy began with Tituba.

Inquiries into Things Dark and Evil

The presence of two slaves in the Parris parsonage—the coarse John Indian and his seemingly ageless spouse, Tituba, reputed to be half black and half Carib—lent an added aspect of prestige to the Parris household. Only the more influential families owned slaves. The Reverend Parris assigned the pair, both carryovers from his Barbados venture, to the heavier, less desirable household tasks.

When not working in the field, John tended the livestock and maintained the woodlot. Parris occasionally hired out John to bear a hand in Deacon Nathaniel Ingersoll's ordinary (a tavern or eating place serving regular meals), which was located diagonally across the road from the parsonage.

Tituba reluctantly took on such chores as boiling and pounding the linens during seasonal wash days, carting water from the well, emptying the slops, scrubbing and sanding the floors, and whatever other inside jobs needed doing. Never an exponent of hard work, Tituba availed herself of any opportunity to interrupt her work schedule and idle the time away with the children. "She found subtle ways of easing her lot," writes Marion L. Starkey, "and one of these was idling with the little girls."

Thus Tituba's influence over youthful Salemites began innocently enough with occasional storytelling work breaks during the day, soon extending into nightly reminiscences of her Barbados upbringing. With the children snuggled up to the fireplace, for the heat from the fire dissipated after only a few feet, Tituba whiled away the cold November nights, recalling wondrous tales and reciting nonsense rhymes from her past. Her stories awed and delighted her young audience, which at first comprised Elizabeth Parris, Abigail Williams, and two other Parris children, a ten-year-old boy and a five-year-old girl (neither of whom played a significant role in the events that followed).

Since the Reverend Parris and his wife, also Elizabeth, spent much of their time among parishioners outside the home, most of Tituba's storytelling sessions went unsupervised. Such lapses of parental guidance emboldened Tituba to further amaze her young listeners with remembered tricks, spells, and voodoo chantings.

Notwithstanding their youthful naïveté, it seems clear that Betty and Abigail must have shared a sense of wrongdoing for taking part in what degenerated into nightly inquiries into things dark and evil. Little is known about Betty's reactions to Tituba's

A Puritan encounters the bizarre-looking Tituba.

revelations, but historical accounts suggest that the bolder Abigail actively urged Tituba to reveal more and more of her macabre knowledge.

Betty and Abigail

Nine-year-old Betty Parris—described by Marion L. Starkey as "a sweet, biddable little girl, ready to obey anyone who spoke with conviction, including to her misfortune, her playmate Abigail"— feared God—and worse, the devil and eternal damnation. Her fears grew naturally out of a constant exposure to the unrelenting railings of her preacher father. Sin, and the vileness of sinners, formed the sum and soul of the Reverend Samuel Parris's sermons:

> I am to make difference between the clean and the unclean, so as to labor to cleanse and purge the one and confirm and strengthen the other. . . . Sinners see no hell, and therefore they fear none. Oh sinners! time enough, time enough, have but a little patience, and you shall see an hell time enough, wrath will overtake you time enough, if you prevent it not by true repentance.

When the Reverend Parris preached one of his fiery sermons, people listened, half in fear of his menacing figure in the pulpit—tall, dressed in basic black, with near-matching dark-brown eyes and a huge jutting chin—and half mesmerized by the tenor of his booming delivery. Parris's bombast intimidated all but a few of his congregation, so young Betty could hardly be expected to feel less timorous. Eleven-year-old Abigail Williams was another matter.

Marion L. Starkey writes:

> She was of a robuster sort, and though as relentlessly catechized [schooled in religion] as her small cousin, instinctively took damnation, death, and most other unpleasant things as something scheduled to happen to someone else, particularly to people she didn't like.

The long-legged, coltish Abigail exhibited a stiffer will and more adventuresome spirit than her younger cousin. Her own salvation, she seemed to feel, was her guaranteed inheritance as a child of the elect (those chosen by divine favor). With her perception of assured deliverance, Abigail likely felt less fear than fascination for the devil and his disciples.

"It would be going too far to say that Abigail loved the devil," Starkey surmises.

> For all her bold spirit, she sometimes quailed before him and had bad dreams. Nevertheless she took a horrid fascination in hearing about him, and while Betty beside her twitched and swallowed her sobs, Abigail leaned forward to catch every word on this subject.

Unsurprisingly, then, Abigail took the lead in encouraging Tituba to delve deeper and deeper into mystic lore. But both girls felt equally repressed by the rigors of Puritanism; and both girls

Tituba, looking wild, exotic, and much older than she would have been in real life, entertains Salem girls with supernatural tales of her native land.

sought relief from pent-up youthful energies born out of a winter's boredom. An explosive release of tensions grew imminent.

The Pangs of Guilt

The girls soon became aware that they were treading on forbidden ground and vowed to keep Tituba's tales to themselves. Betty, the more conscience-driven of the two girls, began to suffer torment and guilt from keeping their activities secret from their elders. As Starkey points out:

> One cannot pursue forbidden pleasures without paying a penalty, without suffering the consequences of a conflict between conscience (or at least fear of discovery) and the unhallowed [unholy] craving. This was true of all the girls, but particularly of little Betty.

Within the narrow construct of Puritan belief, even children came under the constant threat of hellfire. Cotton Mather, the leading and most venerated Boston minister, wrote: "Are the souls of your children of no value? . . . They are not too little to die, they are not too little to go to hell." Later, in a preface to a children's book, he warned:

Do you dare to run up and down upon the Lord's day? Or do you keep in to read your book? . . . They which lie, must go to their father the devil, into everlasting burning; they which never pray, God will pour out his wrath upon them; and when they beg and pray in

In his sermons, Boston minister Cotton Mather reinforced the strict rules of behavior expected of Puritans.

hell fire, God will not forgive them, but there [they] must lie forever. Are you willing to go to hell to be burnt with the devil and his angels? . . . Oh, hell is a terrible place, that's worse a thousand times than whipping.

The prevalence of such heady reminders of the consequences of sin clearly illustrates that Puritan elders hardly shied from the use of terror and shame to encourage proper discipline in their young. Little wonder, then, that sensitive or thoughtful children should feel keenly the pangs of guilt upon their slightest deviation from the Puritans' stark credo of belief and behavior.

The Circle Expands

The older Abigail, according to Starkey, "knew more explicitly than Betty that what she was doing was none of God's work; even her heart may have known its secret pangs of guilt." But she accepted whatever guilt she felt as a stimulant to further exploration. The girls' compulsion to learn more about other-worldly entities drew both of them back each night to Tituba and a warm place before the fire. And despite their vow of secrecy, the girls could not for long keep from sharing their newly learned knowledge of the netherworld with their friends.

Tituba's circle of girls began to expand. Ann Putnam Jr., age twelve, who lived a mile away at farmer Thomas Putnam's, became the first of the girls' companions to join them regularly at the Parrises' hearth. Mary Walcott, sixteen, daughter of Captain Jonathan Walcott, who lived only a few hundred yards away, followed. Next, from a distance of a half mile, came Elizabeth Hubbard, seventeen, great-niece of the aging Dr. and Mrs. Griggs. Susan Sheldon, a newcomer from Maine, and new recruit Elizabeth Booth, both eighteen, joined next. Then Mercy Lewis, nineteen, who resided with the Putnams. And, finally, Mary Warren, twenty, servant of successful tavern owner John Proctor. Tituba's circle had rapidly expanded to encompass nine girls.

Dark Rumors

In January 1692 the excitement generated by the girls' covert explorations into the occult got out of hand. Betty Parris and

BEWITCHED BEHAVIOR

In his scholarly work *Entertaining Satan: Witchcraft and the Culture of Early New England,* history professor John Putnam Demos describes the most commonly documented features of the bewitched teenaged girls:

Preliminaries: The victim becomes anxiously preoccupied with her spiritual condition. She discovers ominous signs of God's displeasure toward her—this in spite of her manifest involvement in religious devotions and her outwardly faultless behavior.

Onset: Her fits begin with spells of fainting, hysterical crying, disordered speech, and disturbances of speech and hearing.

Intensification: The fits become longer, more frequent, and more bizarre in their substantive features. This phase often includes a delusionary confrontation with spectral witches [with the victim] reviling the witches. . . .

Acute Phase: The fits at peak intensity may include the following elements: (1) excruciating sensations of "pricking" or "pinching" (as if by numberless pins and nails), also of "burning" (by invisible flames); (2) bizarre contortions of body parts: twisting, stretching, unusual postures of extreme rigidity and limberness by turns; (3) frenzied motor activity: rolling on the ground, running about aimlessly, simulated "flying" and "diving"; occasional "barking" or other animal imitation; some impulse to injury of self or others; (4) periods of extreme immobility, amounting to paralysis; feelings of extraordinary pressure on the chest or elsewhere; (5) anorexia: more or less complete inhibitions of eating (sometimes accompanied by a strong wish to eat, but with clenching of mouth whenever food is brought); (6) occasional forced consumption of invisible (and painful or poisonous) liquids when overpowered by the witch; (7) "frolicsome" intervals, mostly without pain; cavorting in a "ludicrous" way, babbling impertinent nonsense; insults and gestures of physical assault toward bystanders, friends, and family.

Intermissions: The victim experiences "quiet" periods, lasting hours or days, and characterized by lassitude [weariness or boredom], a "melancholy" air, and feelings of self-reproach.

Professor Demos points out that "these behaviors constitute a package, a syndrome, a composite picture of a considerable group, which partly reflects the individual experience of each victim, while entirely representing none of them."

Abigail Williams began acting strangely. They suffered convulsions and babbled incoherently. In one of her fits, Abigail reached into the fireplace and flung flaming sticks about the parsonage. The girls appeared to be bewitched by something. Some of the other girls joined Betty and Abigail in fits of thrashing and sobbing.

Their symptoms were disturbingly reminiscent of those described in a book written three years earlier by Cotton Mather. In *Memorable Providences Relating to Witchcrafts and Possessions*, the scholarly clergyman recounted the case of a thirteen-year-old young woman named Martha, the eldest daughter of the Goodwin family of Boston.

Martha's affliction had started in the summer of 1688 after some family linen had turned up missing. Martha accused the laundry girl of stealing the linen, whereupon the girl's mother, Mary Glover, "a scandalous old woman," defended her daughter and "bestowed very bad language" upon Martha. According to Mather, Martha began at once to have "strange fits, beyond those that attend an epilepsy or catalepsy."

Shortly thereafter Martha's sister and two brothers fell victim to the same fits in the same parts of the body. When one child was attacked, the siblings immediately experienced equal symptoms. Upon consultation, doctors diagnosed witchcraft as the only possible cause of such symptoms, which Mather described in detail:

Sometimes they would be deaf, sometimes dumb, some-

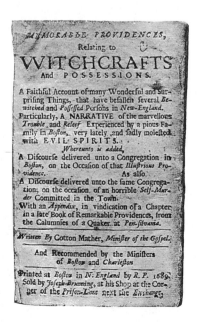

The title page of Cotton Mather's book describing symptoms of witchcraft and possession.

times blind, and often, all at once. One while their tongues would be drawn down their throats, another while they would be pulled out upon their chins, to a prodigious length. They would have their mouths open unto such a wideness, that their jaws went out of joint; and anon [soon] they would clap together again with a force like a strong spring-lock. The same would happen to their shoulder blades, and their elbows, and their hand wrists, and several of their joints. They would at times lie in a benumbed condition; and be drawn together as those that are tied neck and heels; and presently be stretched out, yes, drawn backwards, to such a degree it was feared the very skin of their bellies would have cracked. They would make most piteous outcries, that they were cut with knives, and struck with blows that they could not bear. Their necks would be broken, so that their neck bone would seem dissolved into them that felt after it; and yet on the sudden, it would become again so stiff that there was no stirring of their heads; yes, their heads would be twisted almost round; and if main force at any time obstructed a dangerous motion which they seemed to be upon, they would roar exceedingly. Thus they lay some weeks, most pitiful spectacles.

Mary Glover eventually confessed to being a witch—possibly under duress—and was tried and hanged in Boston. The weird antics of Betty and Abigail, so startlingly similar to those of the Goodwin children, sparked a renewed interest in Cotton Mather's *Memorable Providences*. Dark rumors began to spread like a common cold in Salem Village.

Salem Town and Salem Village

Salem Village, today the independent inland town of Danvers and (ironically) site of a state mental health facility, formed a part of the adjacent port of Salem Town to the southeast in 1692.

Appearances and lifestyles contrasted greatly in the two Salems. The town reflected the wealth of a prosperous seaport in its majestic municipal buildings, fine shops, and grand merchants'

Beneath the idyllic pastoral setting of Salem Village lay greed, superstition, and fear.

homes. The village consisted of a few scattered farmhouses and farms, a town meetinghouse, a parsonage, a tavern, and a handful of tradesmen's dwellings, such as potters, carpenters, and cobblers. Forests and uncharted wilderness all but surrounded the village, which stood separated from the town by rivers and inlets and a walking distance of some two to three hours.

In marked difference to one another, the citizens of Salem Town enjoyed the yields of a bustling trade and the comforts of urban living, while the folks of Salem Village struggled to exist off the land and survive in a frontier setting. Historian Carol F. Karlsen identifies a major source of continuing litigations between the two communities:

> The main issues that split these communities were: when and how men could pass on their property, an issue that divided fathers and sons; whether power and authority would continue to reside in a religious and landed elite or be grasped by a newly risen, religiously diverse mercantile elite; and finally to what degree economic and to some extent political power was to be

shared between the lower-and-middling ranks and the upper-and-middling ranks of men. . . .

Men occasionally expressed their discontent with their place in the hierarchical social order, but when they did they always invited the reprisals of their superiors. . . . Short of revolt, they lived daily with the tension created by their own internal conflicts and resentment of their economic plight.

Though women . . . shared similar tensions, men had much more at stake in their social system, for within it economic power was a male prerogative.

Such divided interests and ever-present tensions fueled the fires of unending legal disputes over property rights and boundary limits. But the two communities shared a common belief in the superstitions of their time and never for a moment questioned the presence and influence of Satan in their lives. The devil in Massachusetts was *real*.

A Wellspring of Fear

Some evidence points to the scary egg-in-the-glass episode as having brought on the girls' first hysterical fits. John Hale, a pastor in neighboring Beverly who soon became involved in the strange phenomena, later would write:

I knew one of the afflicted persons [probably Abigail], who (as I was credibly informed), did try with an egg and a glass to find her future husband's calling; till there came up a coffin, that is, a specter in likeness of a coffin. And she was afterward followed with a diabolical molestation to her death, and so died a single person—a just warning to others to take heed of handling the Devil's weapons lest they get a wound thereby.

Ripples of apprehension radiated from Tituba's circle—by then a wellspring of fear—and the God-fearing people of Salem Village started searching for the cause of the girls' strange affliction.

Chapter 2

First Accusations

BETTY'S AND ABIGAIL'S CONDITIONS worsened as the weeks wore on. The Parrises called several doctors to the parsonage, but the doctors could do nothing. So far, according to Samuel Parris, the possibility of witchcraft involvement had gone unmentioned. "When these calamities first began," the Reverend Parris wrote, "which was in my own family, the affliction was several weeks before such hellish operations as witchcraft were suspected."

Bewitched

About mid-February Dr. William Griggs—the great-uncle of seventeen-year-old Elizabeth Hubbard—conducted yet another examination of Betty and Abigail in his office. He peered at the girls' twitching bodies, poked and prodded them a bit, and consulted his medical books for matching symptoms. After ruling out all known possibilities, he declared the girls to be "under an evil hand."

Modern medicine would almost surely diagnose the convulsions and antics displayed by the girls of old Salem Village as hysteria or conversion reaction. The symptoms can reasonably be attributed to the girls' anxiety over being discovered, as well as their guilt at keeping secrets from their elders. Doctors today have observed similar symptoms in victims of childhood beatings and sexual abuse. But the happenings in Salem Village were of a time when physicians perceived such symptoms as being, in John Hale's words, "beyond the power of . . . natural disease to

As a young woman swoons under the influence of witchcraft, pilgrims pray to cast out the evil spirits afflicting her.

effect." To a medical community steeped in medieval superstition, it seemed clear that the afflicted girls were bewitched.

Witch's Cake

On February 25, 1692, Mary Sibley, Mary Walcott's aunt, took the first step toward learning who or what was afflicting the girls. She approached Reverend Parris's Caribbean servants, John Indian and his wife, Tituba, and asked them to prepare a witch's cake. They complied and baked a cake of meal mixed with the girls' urine. This concoction was fed to the Parrises' dog in the belief that the presence of witchery would be confirmed if the dog began to act strangely. (It was thought that the dog was a familiar—a messenger of the devil assigned to a witch.) No records exist as to what happened to the dog.

When the Reverend Parris heard about Mary Sibley's witch cake activity several weeks later, he was appalled and denounced her experiment from the pulpit as "going to the Devil for help against the Devil." He both privately admonished Mary about it and before the entire congregation summoned her "to deep humiliation for what she has done." Mary Sibley cried and confessed her sins, but too late. The cake had been baked and the damage done. "The Devil has been raised among us," Parris preached with his usual fervor, "and his rage is vehement and terrible; and, when he shall be silenced, the Lord only knows."

Shortly thereafter the girls, their confidence apparently bolstered by Mary Sibley's confession, started identifying those responsible for their distress, initially naming three women. At that point, Joseph Hutchinson, Thomas Putnam, Edward Putnam, and Thomas Preston—four "yeomen of Salem Village in the County of Essex"—appeared before their magistrates and swore out complaints of witchcraft against the three women.

On February 29, warrants for arrest were issued against Sarah Good, Sarah Osborne, and Tituba. The three accused witches were taken to the Salem Village meetinghouse the following day to be examined by magistrates John Hathorne (the great-great-grandfather of Nathaniel Hawthorne, who added a "w" to the name) and Jonathan Corwin. "Magistrate Hathorne led the questioning," writes author Richard Marshall, "not in the manner of impartial inquiry, but in the style of a prosecuting attorney, and his questions . . . clearly assumed his respondent's guilt."

A Perfect Target

Sarah Good, the first alleged witch to face the magistrates and her accusers, was thirty-nine years old. But to neighbors—who somehow overlooked Sarah's pregnancy and her four-and-a-half year-old daughter Dorcas—she looked closer to seventy. Through a series of misfortunes, Sarah had been reduced to poverty and forced to beg for her survival.

Sarah's woes began in 1672, when her father, John Solart, a prosperous Wenham innkeeper, committed suicide, thereby disgracing his family in Puritan eyes. Wenham was one of several peripheral towns engaged in ongoing feuds with Salem Village over land grants and boundaries. Sarah's mother gained control of her late husband's estate—worth five hundred pounds—and seventy-seven acres of land, remarried, and refused to share the wealth with any of her seven children. A court granted Sarah a small parcel of land ten years later, but nowhere near her rightful due.

Sarah carried her bad luck into two marriages. She first married Daniel Poole, an indentured servant, who died soon after and left Sarah heavily burdened with his debts. Then she married a laborer named William Good. Sarah's ill fortune persisted. Her first husband's creditors sued her to recover their losses, whereupon the court ordered Sarah to forfeit part of her land in payment. When her new husband could not find work in a sluggish economy, Sarah lost the rest of her property. The couple soon descended into total poverty, forced to beg for food and shelter.

Sarah's scraggly gray hair, stooped body, and line-ridden face, induced in part by hardship, not only belied her age but lent a witchy cast to her appearance. Her raspy voice and surly disposition, also a product of fortune's disfavor, facilitated her haglike perception in the eyes of the community, as did her long-standing habit of pipe smoking. Sarah Good's witchy appearance and irascible behavior, then, plus the fact that she was a woman and a pauper, made her a perfect target for persecution.

Spectral Evidence

Ann Putnam Jr., the third member of Tituba's circle, became the first accuser to take dead aim on the hapless Sarah. In a deposition (sworn statement) Ann testified, in part:

Puritan leaders arrest a woman on suspicion of witchcraft. Scholars point out that it was often elderly women living on their own—and thus outside the protection of men—who were first accused.

[On the 25th of February] I saw the apparition [specter] of Sarah Good, which did torture me most grievously. But I did not know her name until the 27th of February, and then she told me her name was Sarah Good, and then she did prick me and pinch me most grievously, and also since, several times urging me vehemently to write in her [witch's] book.

Ann went on to state that she had seen "the apparition of Sarah Good go and afflict and torture the bodies" of Elizabeth Parris, Abigail Williams, Elizabeth Hubbard, and Sarah Bibber. In a similar deposition, Elizabeth Hubbard echoed Ann's words, adding:

> In the night after Sarah Good's examination, Sarah Good came to me barefoot and barelegged, and did most grievously torment me by pricking and pinching me. And I verily believe that Sarah Good has bewitched me.

According to court secretary Ezekiel Cheever, "the worshipful Assistants John Hathorne [and] Jonathan Curran [Corwin]" conducted Sarah Good's examination on March 1. Hathorne, who had apparently prejudged Sarah, relied heavily on bullying tactics to force her confession:

HATHORNE: Sarah Good, what evil spirit have you familiarity with?

GOOD: None.

H: Have you made no contract with the devil?

G: No.

H: Why do you hurt these children?

G: I do not hurt them. I scorn it.

H: Who do you employ, then, to do it?

G: I employ nobody.

H: What creature do you employ then?

G: No creature. But I am falsely accused.

H: Why did you go away muttering from Mr. Parris's house? [She had called children vile names while begging at Parris's house and had walked away mumbling to herself. The children fell ill and experienced fits a short time later.]

G: I did not mutter, but I thanked him for what he gave my child.

H: Have you made no contract with the Devil?

G: No.

Hathorne then interrupted Sarah's questioning and directed several young girls present at the hearing to look at Sarah Good "and see if this were the person who had hurt them." The girls—Ann Putnam, Elizabeth Hubbard, and others of Tituba's circle—looked at Sarah and confirmed that she was indeed their tormentor, then immediately plunged into convulsions. When they recovered, the girls claimed that Sarah Good, although physically removed from them, had tormented them "spectrally."

This so-called spectral evidence, that is, evidence based on the premise that a person possessed by the devil can project his or her image—unbound by time or space—to torment or harm another, was readily accepted by the examiners. By admitting spectral evidence into the record, the magistrates established a critical precedent for subsequent hearings and trials.

"An Enemy to All Good"

Ezekiel Cheever concluded the record of Sarah Good's examination with his opinionated observations of her demeanor and a brief recounting of William Good's damning testimony against his wife:

> Her answers were in a very wicked, spiteful manner, reflecting and retorting against the authority with base and abusive words, and many lies she was taken in.

> It was here said that her husband had said that he was afraid that she either was a witch or would be one very quickly. The worshipful Mr. Hathorne asked him his reason why he said so of her, whether he had ever seen anything by her. He answered no, not in this nature, but it was her bad carriage to him. And indeed, said he, I may say with tears [and with no pun intended] that she is an enemy to all good.

The worshipful assistants Hathorne and Corwin must have felt that they had heard enough. They ordered Sarah Good removed and asked for Sarah Osborne to be brought in.

As Sarah Good was being led out, she railed, "It is Gammer [Sarah] Osborne that did pinch and afflict the children." She was temporarily held in Ingersoll's ordinary, where she sat calmly puffing on her pipe, awaiting transport to jail.

A woman under suspicion of witchcraft is examined for moles and blemishes, signs that, to her Puritan persecutors, would prove that she is a witch.

The Puritan Heart

Sarah Osborne, a sixty-nine-year-old invalid, followed Sarah Good to the stand. She brought to the hearings a background not unlike that of her predecessor. Widowed by the death of her prosperous and politically active first husband, Robert Prince—owner of a 150-acre farm and other holdings along the disputed Salem Village–Topsfield boundary—Sarah had married her indentured servant John Osborne. Together, the Osbornes tried to change Prince's will.

Prince had stipulated that Sarah was to handle his estate until his two sons (six and two years old at the time) came of age, at which time the land would become theirs. To ensure that his sons received their inheritance, Prince appointed his neighbors, who were also his in-laws, Thomas and John Putnam, to supervise Sarah's handling of the trust. The Putnams took more than a casual interest in Sarah Osborne's hearing, which closely paralleled Sarah Good's examination.

The two Sarahs claimed a further affinity in that neither woman attended church, albeit for different reasons. The impoverished Sarah Good testified that she stayed away from God's house "for want of cloose [clothes]!" The old, disabled, and bedridden Sarah Osborne was simply physically unable to attend services. Poverty and infirmity rarely stirred compassion in the Puritan heart, however, and were far more likely to earn contempt.

Familiar Fits

Hathorne's questioning of Sarah Osborne repeated the same line that he had used with Sarah Good. He asked about her familiarity with evil spirits, whether she had made a pact with the devil, and suchlike. Osborne, like Good, denied everything. Hathorne suddenly veered off in a new direction and asked her how well she knew Sarah Good. She answered initially that she had not seen Good for two years and had not then known her name, in an apparent effort to distance herself from another witch suspect. But Hathorne pressured her until she finally admitted that she had in fact called Sarah Good by her name when they met two years ago.

Hathorne's somewhat vague strategy became clear when he announced, "Sarah Good says it was you that hurt the children."

Osborne denied Good's charge, insisting, "I do not know that the devil goes about in my likeness to do any hurt." Hathorne, according to the court recorder, again interrupted the hearing:

> Mr. Hathorne desired all the children to stand up and look upon her and see if they did know her which they all did and every one of them said that this was one of the women that did afflict them and that they had constantly seen her in the very habit [clothes] that she was now in.

Following their identification of Osborne, the girls, as if on cue, fell once again into their all too familiar fits.

Dark Regions

Deodat Lawson, a minister and witness to many such demonstrations, later took a hard look at whether the girls' actions were purely voluntary. He wrote:

> Sometimes, in their fits, they have had their tongues drawn out of their mouths to a fearful length, their heads turned very much over their shoulders; and while they have been so strained in their fits, and had their arms and legs, etc., wrested as if they were quite dislocated, the blood has gushed out of their mouths for a considerable time together, which some, so that they might be satisfied that it was real blood, took upon their finger, and rubbed on their other hand. I saw several together thus violently strained and bleeding in their fits, to my very great astonishment that my fellow mortals should be so grievously distressed by the invisible powers of darkness. For certainly all considerate persons who beheld these things must needs be convinced, that their motions in their fits were preternatural [existing outside of nature or inexplicable by ordinary means] and involuntary, both as to the manner, which was so strange as a well person could not (at least not without great pain) screw their bodies into, and as to violence also, they were preternatural motions, being much beyond the ordinary force of the same persons when they were in their right minds.

Clearly, forces beyond the girls' ordinary mental and physical capabilities enabled the girls to perform in such an extraordinary way. Puritan thinking attributed those forces to powers assigned to witches by the devil himself. Today's thinking might be more inclined to root the causes of such antics in the dark regions of the human psyche.

Sufficient Cause

Apparently shaken by the girls' screaming and choking, and aware that her defense of merely denying their accusations wasn't working, Sarah tried to align herself with the afflicted

As an accused witch proclaims her innocence, one of the possessed girls begins to convulse in a hysterical fit.

girls. She called attention to her present state of ill health and said that she was more likely to be bewitched than to be a witch. She told Hathorne, according to the court record, that "she was frightened one time in her sleep and either saw or dreamed that she saw a thing like an Indian, all black, which did pinch her in her neck and pulled her by the back part of her head to the door of the house." Hathorne asked if she had ever seen anything else and she answered no.

Several spectators then cried out that she had said "she would never be tied to that lying spirit any more." Hathorne snapped at this:

HATHORNE: What lying spirit is this? Has the Devil ever deceived you and been false to you?

OSBORNE: I do not know the Devil. I never did see him.

H: What lying spirit was it then?

O: It was a voice that I thought I heard.

H: What did it propound to you?

O: That I should go no more to [church] meeting. But I said I would, and did go the next Sabbath Day.

But the testimony of her husband and others contradicted Sarah. "She had not been at meeting," they said, "this year and two months." Her failure to attend church, coupled with her vision of the "Indian, all black," and her mutterings of a "lying spirit," gave the magistrates sufficient cause to hold Sarah Osborne for trial. They dismissed her and called for Tituba to be brought before them.

Tituba Confesses

Tituba's examination represented, in today's words, the main event on that first day of March. Her interrogation by Hathorne began routinely but quickly changed. She denied having familiarity with evil spirits or hurting the children. Hathorne persisted:

HATHORNE: Who is it then?
TITUBA: The Devil, for all I know. [Hathorne took her answer to mean that she *knew* it was the devil.]

H: What appearance or how does he appear when he hurts them, with what shape or what is he like that hurts them?

T: Like a man, I think yesterday . . . I saw a thing like a man.

The room fell silent. Tituba admitted to an acquaintance with the devil, whom she described as a tall man in black, with white hair, but who sometimes appeared as an animal. "The Devil came to me and bid me serve him," she said.

Tituba spoke of making her mark of agreement in red in the devil's book, which had nine names in it, including those of Sarah Good and Sarah Osborne. She declared that the two Sarahs had hurt the children and had wanted her to do the same. The crowd hung on her every word. Even the afflicted girls kept still. Warming to their attention, Tituba further confessed that

In this fanciful depiction, Tituba, looking decidely odd and witchlike, threatens a newcomer to Salem. At her hearing, she confessed to being a witch.

she often saw Good and Osborne in company with the devil and two Boston witches whose names she didn't know. And she admitted once pinching Ann Putnam and Elizabeth Hubbard but refusing to do so a second time.

At Hathorne's bidding, she variously described the first one to hurt the children as a man, a hog, and a great black dog, implying that all were forms of the devil. Tituba additionally disclosed that Sarah Good had two familiars, a cat and a yellow bird. Sarah Osborne also had a pair of familiars, one with wings, two legs, and a head like a woman; the other "all over hairy, all the face hairy and a long nose and I don't know how to tell how the face looks, with two legs, it . . . is about two or three feet high and goes upright like a man and last night it stood before the fire in Mr. Parris's hall."

Perhaps Tituba's most startling revelation came when Hathorne asked how she and the two Sarahs had traveled to the homes of the afflicted girls. "I rid upon a stick or pole and Good and Osborne behind me," she answered. "We ride taking hold of one another." The afflicted girls again went into fits.

Hathorne asked Tituba who was afflicting them, and she named Sarah Good. The girls agreed. Then Elizabeth Hubbard was taken with an even worse fit. Hathorne again asked Tituba to name the tormentor, but this time she could not. "I am blind now," she said. "I cannot see." She then herself fell into convulsions.

Only the Beginning

Seventeenth-century superstition held that once a witch had renounced her calling she could no longer "see." Of Tituba's sudden blindness and subsequent descent into convulsions, author and journalist Frances Hill writes:

> No doubt she hoped, by joining the girls in their afflictions, to avoid being jailed as a possible afflicter. But her hope was in vain. Hathorne decreed that Good, Osborne, and Tituba must all be examined further and sent them to jail.

Sarah Good, Sarah Osborne, and Tituba were examined again on March 3 and 5. On March 7, the three women were remanded to custody in Boston jail to await trial. The first witch examinations had ended, but the witch-hunts were just beginning.

Chapter 3

Shadow over Salem Village

THE CONVULSIVE ANTICS THAT STARTED WITH Betty Parris and Abigail Williams had spread outwardly on the widening ripples of Tituba's circle. By the end of February, at least two other young girls—probably Ann Putnam Jr. and Elizabeth Hubbard—had joined Betty and Abigail in experiencing fits and seeing visions. Similar ills beset Mary Walcott and Mercy Lewis soon thereafter.

Brother Against Brother

On March 3, in the middle of the first witch hearings, young Ann Putnam had reported seeing the apparition of Goody Proctor in company with the specters of Good, Osborne, and Tituba. ("Goody" was the short form for "Goodwife," an archaic title for the mistress of a household.) Ann claimed that Goody Proctor had bit, pinched, and nearly choked her.

John Proctor, Goodwife Proctor's husband, was a successful landowner, tavern keeper, and businessperson who lived on the outskirts of Salem Town. He had never involved himself with Salem Village politics or boundary disputes, but, as a latecomer to the village in 1666, he had never gained favor with the influential Putnam family. Of greater import, perhaps, he had publicly voiced doubts about the validity of the girls' fits and the legitimacy of the witch hearings. And John's wife was heard to agree with him. Within a month, Goodwife Proctor was called upon to answer witch charges. Husband John rose to her defense and found himself facing similar charges.

Joseph Putnam, a younger, estranged half-brother of Thomas, numbered himself (as did the Proctors) among the more skeptical townsfolk. He preferred practical rather than mystical explanations for the afflicted girls' odd behavior. When Joseph heard that Thomas's daughter was starting to predict the future and make further witch accusations, he hastened to his brother's house and reportedly told the girl's mother: "If you dare to touch with your foul lies anyone belonging to my household, you will answer for it!" Witch mania had already escalated to the point of pitting brother against brother.

A Member of the Church

At about this time, the Parrises sent nine-year-old Betty off to Salem Town to stay with Stephen Sewell and his family. They perhaps felt that her young age exposed her more than the older girls to mental and physical harm from the continuing fits. Betty's fits gradually subsided. Then, after supposedly purifying her conscience by confessing to the Reverend John Hale about the illicit prophesying sessions with Tituba, her symptoms disappeared completely. If the Parrises had thought as much of Abigail as they did of their daughter, they might have sent her away as well.

And if some of the other parents and guardians of Salem Village had thought more of their children's well-being and less of contesting property rights and boundaries, they might have taken measures to separate the girls long enough to see whether the fits might subside. But they did not, and the girls continued to meet regularly at one another's homes, in the meetinghouse, and at Ingersoll's tavern.

On March 11, 1692, the citizens of Salem Village observed a day of prayer and fasting. Ministers from all around Essex County gathered at the Reverend Samuel Parris's parsonage to consult with him and to pray for his distressed parishioners. The afflicted girls joined in the prayer sessions. A contemporary account of that "solemn day of prayer," written seven years later by a Boston merchant named Robert Calef, described the girls as being

> for the most part silent, but after any one prayer was ended, they would act and speak strangely and ridiculously, yet were such as had been well educated and of good behavior, the one, a girl of eleven or twelve years old [either Abigail Williams or Ann Putnam] would sometimes seem to be in a convulsion fit, her limbs being twisted several ways, and very stiff, but presently her fit would be over.

The fasting and prayers did little to alleviate or put an end to the girls' afflictions. Before the day was out, the girls "cried out on" (accused) Martha Corey, a respectable, sixty-five-year-old matron and member in good standing of the church at Salem Village.

A Fatal Mistake

Nineteenth-century historian W. Elliot Woodward wrote that upon hearing Ann's latest accusation on March 12, Edward Putnam and Ezekiel Cheever, two of Martha Corey's fellow church members, decided that it was their "duty to go to her and see what she would

say to this complaint, she being in church covenant with us." It seems reasonable to assume that Edward, brother of Thomas Putnam and uncle of Ann, and Ezekiel Cheever, the less than objective court reporter at the first witch hearings, might have had something other than Martha's best interests at heart.

Giles Corey hammers a horseshoe in a doorway to bring luck. The elderly Corey's wife, Martha, was accused of witchcraft.

Before they left from Thomas's house that morning, they asked young Ann what Martha was wearing, supposedly to verify that she had made no mistake in her identification. But Ann maintained that Martha, after hearing of the two men's intended visit, had blinded her. Oddly, no one thought it strange that Martha would blind Ann to the sight of her specter and then identify herself.

Martha was the third wife of eighty-one-year-old Giles Corey, the contrary owner of one hundred valuable acres of land near the Ipswich River. She was alone in her house just over the line from Salem Village in Salem Town when Putnam and Cheever arrived.

Highly opinionated, always right, and never averse to making her views known, Goodwife Corey also had an annoying habit of trying to put words in the mouths of others. These traits added little to her popularity in the community. Nor did the fact that she had once borne an illegitimate mulatto child enhance her image with her peers. Although a woman of some wealth, fully integrated into the Salem Village community, Martha's reputation was somewhat less than bright and shining.

Martha greeted the two men with a smile, Cheever wrote later, and said, "I know what you are come for; you are come to talk with me about being a witch, but I am none. I cannot help people's talking of me." Cheever further wrote:

> Edward Putnam answered her that it was the afflicted person that did complain of her that was the occasion of our coming to her. She presently replied, "But does she tell you what clothes I have on?" We made her no answer to this at first asking, whereupon she asked again with very great eagerness, "But does she tell you what clothes I have on?" . . . Which questions, with the eagerness of mind with which she did ask, made us to think of what Ann Putnam had told us before we went to her, and we told her no, she did not, for she told us that you came and blinded her and told her that she should see no more before it was night, that so she might not tell us what

clothes you had on. She made but little answer to this but seemed to smile at it, as if she had showed us a pretty trick.

It is not clear how Martha Corey knew that they would try to identify her by her clothes. Speculation suggests that she must have learned it from someone who had been present at the Thomas Putnam house that morning. Regardless of how she learned about it, Martha's strategy of confronting Putnam and Cheever with her knowledge of their intent, that is, her "pretty trick," turned out to be a fatal mistake, as she soon discovered.

The Yellow Bird

A warrant for Martha Corey's arrest was issued late in the day on Saturday, March 19, upon the complaint of Edward Putnam and a friend. The complaint charged that Martha had "done much hurt and injury" to Ann Putnam, Ann Putnam Jr., Mercy Lewis, Elizabeth Hubbard, and Abigail Williams. With their latest accusations, the girls had moved above poverty's lot for the first time in choosing an affluent matron as victim of their slurs.

Because her arrest warrant had been issued too late to be served on Saturday, and could not be served on the Sabbath, Martha Corey remained free until Monday, March 21, which enabled her to attend church on Sunday. At least seven of the afflicted persons, including newcomers Mrs. Gertrude Pope and Goodwife Sarah Bibber, were also in attendance.

Reverend Deodat Lawson preached sermons at both the morning and afternoon services on Sunday. Lawson, a former Salem Village minister, had come down from Boston to view for himself the witchcraft scourge that was plaguing his former parish. Also, on a more personal note, the afflicted girls were saying that Lawson's wife and daughter, who died three years earlier, had been murdered by "infernal powers." This information alone would seem sufficient to inspire the theme of his sermon, entitled "Christ's Fidelity the Only Shield Against Satan's Malignity."

The afflicted girls reacted to the good pastor's preachings by falling at once into fits, as Lawson later described:

They had several sore fits in the time of public worship, which did something [somewhat] interrupt me in my first prayer, being so unusual. After Psalm was sung, Abigail Williams said to me, "Now stand up and name your text." And after it was read she said, "It was a long text." In the beginning of sermon, Mrs. Pope . . . said to me, "Now there is enough of that."

These interruptions sound more like deliberate acts of impudence than involuntary manifestations of tormented souls. The outbursts resumed during the afternoon services:

And in the afternoon, Abigail Williams, upon my referring to my doctrine said to me, "I know no doctrine you had. If you did name one I have forgot it." In sermon time when Goodwife Corey was present in the meetinghouse Abigail Williams called out, "Look where Goodwife Corey sits on the beam, suckling her yellow bird [allegedly her spectral familiar] between her fingers!" Ann Putnam . . . said there was a yellow bird sat on my hat as it hung on the pin in the pulpit, but those that were by [her] restrained her from speaking aloud about it.

A defiant Martha Corey sat steadfastly—even courageously—in her seat throughout the entire service. Her thoughts and feelings about the yellow bird sightings belong to the irrecoverable past.

A Telling Lie

Martha Corey became the fourth woman to face witch charges when she confronted her accusers in the Salem Village meetinghouse on March 21. Worshipful assistant John Hathorne lashed out at her immediately, showing her far less compassion or benefit of the doubt than he had shown the first three witch suspects. "You are now in the hands of authority," he told her coldly, leading in to his interrogation.

HATHORNE: Tell us who hurts these children.

COREY: I do not know.

H: If you be guilty of this fact, do you think you can hide it?

Martha Corey at her trial for witchcraft. As she proclaims her innocence, one of the afflicted girls claims that she is attacking her.

C: The Lord knows.

H: Well, tell us what you know of this matter.

C: Why, I am a gospel woman, and do you think I can have to do with witchcraft too?

H: How could you tell, then, that the child was bid to observe what clothes you wore, when some came to speak with you?

Martha said that Cheever had told her, but he declared that she spoke falsely. She then claimed that she had learned it from her husband, who also denied telling her. Hathorne probed harder:

H: Did you not say your husband told you so? [Martha did not answer, so he went on.] Who hurts these children? Now look upon them.

C: I cannot help it.

H: Did you not say you would tell the truth [about] why you asked the question? How came you to the knowledge?

C: I did but ask.

H: You dare thus to lie in all this assembly! You are now before authority! I expect the truth. You promised it. Speak now, and tell us who told you [about the] clothes.

C: Nobody.

Hathorne kept on in like fashion for much longer, but, to Martha's undoing, he had already caught her in a telling lie.

"You Can't Prove Me a Witch!"

Throughout Martha's testimony, the girls provided background for Hathorne's harsh interrogation, engaging in their usual seizures and impromptu shouts. When Martha occasionally bit her lips while being questioned, or exhibited other nervous mannerisms, the girls complained at various times that Martha was biting, pinching, and strangling them. Reverend Nicholas Noyes, a local pastor, explained the phenomenon as a form of image magic in which Martha used her own body instead of a doll (as in the practice of voodoo) to inflict harm on others.

When Hathorne asked Martha how she had known that she was going to be questioned about the clothes she wore, Mary Walcott and Abigail Williams claimed that they saw a man whispering in her ear. The spectators gasped at the implication that Satan himself was Martha's informant. Hathorne demanded to know more.

H: What did he say to you?

C: We must not believe all that these distracted children say.

H: Cannot you tell what that man whispered?

C: I saw no body.

H: But did not you hear?

C: No.

Martha Corey defiantly proclaims her innocence as she is asked to sign a document saying that she is a witch.

Hathorne abandoned that line of questioning and urged Martha to confess her guilt. She replied, "So I would if I were guilty."

Martha Corey continued to deny all charges against her and held firm in her belief that justice would prevail. As she was being led off to Salem prison to await further examination, she cried, "You can't prove me a witch!" To her eternal misfortune, however, she could not prove that she was not. And the claims of the "distracted" children threatened to weigh more heavily on the justice scales than the denials of an unveiled liar and trickster.

Bad Times and Good People

On the night of his arrival in Salem Village on March 19, the Reverend Deodat Lawson had paid a friendly visit to the parsonage of his fellow minister Samuel Parris. While he was there, Abigail Williams fell into a "grievous fit," as Lawson reported later.

She ran hither and yon, flapping her arms wildly like a flightless bird attempting to take wing, crying, "Whish! Whish! Whish!" Abigail then claimed to see Goodwife Rebecca Nurse,

SOME INFECTIOUS ILLNESS

On Wednesday, March 23, 1692, Reverend Deodat Lawson visited the home of Thomas Putnam to inquire about Putnam's ailing wife, Ann Sr. The elder Ann had been suffering for several days from the biting, pricking, and pinching of witches, allegedly tormented first by the specter of Martha Corey and then by that of Rebecca Nurse. Ann, in a rational moment, asked Lawson to pray for her. He obliged her, "though the apparition said [probably as reported by Ann], I should not." Lawson went on to describe the bedside prayer session:

> At the first beginning she attended; but after a little time, was taken with a fit: yet continued silent, and seemed to be asleep: when prayer was done, her husband going to her, found her in a fit: he took her off the bed, to set her on her knees; but at first she was so stiff, she could not be bended; but she afterwards set down; but quickly began to strive violently with her arms and legs; she then began to complain of, and as it were to converse personally with, Goodwife Nurse, saying, "Goodwife Nurse be gone! Be gone! Be gone! Are you not ashamed, a woman of your profession, to afflict a poor creature so? what hurt did I ever do you in my life! you have but two years to live, and then the devil will torment your soul, for this your name is blotted out of God's book, and shall never be put in God's book again, be gone for shame, are you not afraid of that which is coming upon you? I know, I know, what will make you afraid; the wrath of an angry God, I am sure that will make you afraid; be gone, do not torment me, I know what you would have (we judged she meant, her soul) but it is out of your reach; it is clothed with the white robes of Christ's righteousness."

Ann Putnam Sr., the once-intelligent but by then disturbed mother of Ann Putnam Jr., is said by some to have been the ringleader of the afflicted girls and instigator of many of their accusations. Many of the witch accusations originated with Ann Jr., and her father, Thomas, signed ten of the twenty-one formal complaints issued against accused witches.

Thomas Putnam and Ann Putnam Sr. died in 1699. Thomas was forty-six at death; Ann, thirty-seven. They died within two weeks of each other. It is possible that one or both committed suicide out of guilt for the deaths of twenty innocent people and the pain and hardship inflicted on countless others. It is more probable, however, that they both died of some infectious illness.

a highly respectable seventy-one-year-old church member. "Do you not see her? Why there she stands!"

She next declared that Goody Nurse offered her "the book." Abigail cried out several times, "I won't, I won't, I won't, take it, I do not know what the book is: I am sure it is none of God's book, it is the devil's book, for all I know." She then ran to the fire and began throwing firebrands about the house, then ran back to the fire as if trying to run up the chimney.

Between March 21 and 23, Ann Putnam Sr. joined the circle of afflicted girls in experiencing convulsions. They collectively named as their tormentor the aged, deaf, and sickly Rebecca Nurse, a woman well known for her kindnesses toward others. Soon afterward, Israel and Elizabeth Porter, Rebecca's middle-aged neighbors, paid her a visit to inform her of the girls' claims.

Rebecca had lain sick in bed for eight or nine days but greeted their arrival with warmth and a smile. Before the Porters could broach the subject of their visit, Rebecca asked for news of the afflicted children. "I go to God for them," she said softly, pausing to stare thoughtfully into her little fireplace. "But I am troubled, oh I am troubled at some of their crying out. Some of the persons they have spoken of are, as I believe, as innocent as I." Her virtuous concern for the girls' well-being touched the Porters deeply, but they felt obliged to deliver their disturbing message and did.

Old Rebecca stared for a moment as if in a trance, then said, "Well, if it be so, the will of the Lord be done." She sat for a while in apparent amazement, before adding, "As to this thing I am innocent as the child unborn; but surely, what sin has God found in me unrepented of that He would lay such an affliction on me in my old age?" The Porters, deeply moved, did not reply.

In a later statement in Rebecca's behalf, the Porters wrote: "According to our best observation, we could not discern that she knew what we came for before we told her." Daniel Andrew, a friend of Rebecca's, and Peter Cloyce, husband of Rebecca's sister Sarah, signed as witnesses to the statement. In an atmosphere of witch hysteria, it took great courage to openly support an accused witch. The actions of Rebecca's defenders demonstrated once again that the worst of times often brings out the best in people.

Shape of the Devil

Despite Rebecca's respectable standing in the community, Edward and Jonathan Putnam, young Ann Putnam's uncle and cousin, respectively, swore out a complaint against Rebecca. A warrant for her arrest was issued on March 23 "for vehement suspicion of having committed sundry acts of witchcraft" against Ann Putnam Sr., Ann Putnam Jr., Abigail Williams, and others. Early on the morning of March 24, Marshal George Herrick aroused the still-sleeping, still-ailing Rebecca Nurse, arrested her, and delivered her to the meetinghouse at 10:00 A.M. for examination.

Local opinion as to Rebecca Nurse's guilt was split into two factions. Most of the Putnam clan and their sympathizers, including the Parrises, decried Nurse's guilt; those opposed to the Putnams supported her innocence.

Even magistrate John Hathorne, the brother of Elizabeth Porter, reflected the town's ambivalence as he undertook Rebecca's questioning with misgivings. When he asked her gently to answer the charges against her, she replied in trembling voice, "I can say before my Eternal Father, I am innocent, and God will clear my innocency." Hathorne again spoke gently.

"Here is never a one in the assembly but desires it. But if you be guilty, pray God discover you." He had not exhibited such kindly tone and gentle demeanor in his earlier examinations.

Rebecca's hearing began amid the usual clamor and spasmodic interruptions from the chorus of afflicted girls. Court records show that Henry Kenney testified that when "Nurse came into the house he was seized twice with an amazed condition"; Edward Putnam declared that she had tormented his niece in his presence.

Rebecca responded, "I am innocent and clear and have not been able to get out of doors these eight-nine days," adding, "I never afflicted no child, no, never in my life." The proceeding continued into the afternoon. Rebecca unwaveringly proclaimed her innocence, time and again. Hathorne at last read to her the most serious charge, brought by Ann Putnam Sr., which claimed that Rebecca, with other witches, had murdered several infant children.

"What think you of this?" Hathorne asked.

"I cannot tell what to think of it," she replied. Then, she volunteered a theory that would not soon be forgotten. "The Devil may appear in my shape," she speculated.

A document records Martha Corey's examination at her trial. While the trials had all the trappings of being objective and thorough, the acceptance of the girls' "spectral evidence" made a mockery of the proceedings.

Her speculation bore great significance in that it suggested for the first time that the specters seen by the girls, and which tormented them, could be sent by the devil without the knowledge or consent of the original. Rebecca's theory was apparently lost on the magistrates. At hearing's end, they ordered her imprisoned and held for trial.

Old and Young Alike

Also on March 24, Dorcas Good, Sarah Good's four-and-a-half-year-old daughter, was accused of witchcraft and arrested. Dorcas readily confessed to being a witch. When questioned in her cell by Hathorne, Jonathan Corwin, and John Higginson, a Salem minister, she confessed to owning her own familiar—"a little snake that sucked on the lowest joint of her forefinger." They asked her if the black man (the devil) gave it to her. She said, no, it was a gift from her mother.

Despite her tender years, the magistrates needed little convincing as to Dorcas's witchy status, and they committed her to jail. After serving eight months in a dungeon, starved, and probably chained with the other "witches," Dorcas descended into a lifelong madness.

The spreading witch hysteria in Salem Village cast a dark shadow on the very old and the very young alike. And the shadow was growing longer and darker with each passing day.

Chapter 4

A Glimmer of Hope

WITCH ACCUSATIONS ABOUNDED IN APRIL, followed by examinations and imprisonments. By month's end, the magistrates had sent another twenty-three witch suspects off to jail pending trial. Among them were John and Elizabeth Proctor, Bridget Bishop, Giles Corey, Mary and Phillip English, and George Burroughs. Accusations had spread to include relatives of witches and had moved outside the boundaries of Salem Village to the nearby communities of Beverly, Amesbury, Salem Town, and elsewhere. Four of eleven legal complaints leading to the arrests of the accused had been lodged by Thomas Putnam, father of Ann Putnam Jr., and staunch supporter of Reverend Samuel Parris.

A young woman faces another's accusations that she is a witch.

The Putnam Family

In reviewing the history of the Salem witch trials, it almost seems as if the Putnam family and all their kin made up half the population of Salem Village and its environs. It might also be speculated that the removal of the Putnams might have gone a long way toward forestalling—or at least minimizing—the witch-hunts. Although numerous Putnams participated in the unpleasant scenario, it is perhaps the name of Thomas Putnam—beyond those of the afflicted Anns, senior and junior—that appears most often in accounts of those tragic days. (Thomas was actually a junior but is generally referred to without the distinguishing suffix, as is the case herein.)

Thomas Putnam, husband to Ann Sr. and father to Ann Jr., along with his uncle, Nathaniel Putnam, had led the campaign to install Reverend Samuel Parris as pastor of the Salem Village parish. As champion of Parris's appointment, Thomas must have been appalled when members of his appointee's family appeared to have fallen under the sinister influence of the devil. And it is likely that he agonized even further when his daughter—and later his wife—experienced similar symptoms of the bewitched. Thomas could hardly stand idly by while the devil worked his evil ways, tormenting his loved ones and besmirching his reputation. He took up the sword of righteousness and set forth to smite the devil.

Thomas Putnam's household became the center for witchcraft accusations. And, as some historians believe, Thomas became, if not the driving force behind the witch-hunts, at least one of its chief instigators. Most of the Putnam clan joined Thomas in his determined struggle to avert the shame associated with the bizarre behavior of the afflicted ones. One notable exception was Thomas's half-brother, Joseph Putnam, son of Thomas Putnam Sr. by a second marriage to Mary Veren, and heir to most of the senior Thomas's estate.

The younger Thomas, as firstborn son of his father's first marriage to Ann Holyoke, had fully expected to inherit the bulk of the senior Thomas's three-hundred-acre estate. Instead, he was bequeathed only a small farm on a tiny plot of land, with the remaining acreage going to Joseph. Feelings ran high between the two half-brothers over their father's decision to make Joseph his principal beneficiary. Thomas grew bitterly resentful of Joseph, which eventually led to an unbreachable schism in their relations.

Their fractured relationship resulted in Thomas and Joseph's taking opposite sides in community affairs. Villagers with vested land interests fought hard to keep Salem Village autonomous, while those with mercantile attachments vigorously supported efforts to merge with Salem Town. The politically active and influential Thomas, a prosperous farmer in his own right, favored an independent Salem Village government. Joseph, with commercial ties to Salem Town—through his mother, the widow of an affluent Salem ship captain—strongly opposed town-village separation. Quite naturally, upon the outbreak of afflictions and witchcraft accusations, the gap between the two brothers widened.

Joseph, odd man out of the Putnam clan, soon emerged as the leading figure in the anti-Parris, and thus anti-Putnam, faction in Salem Village. Joseph's principal followers were Joseph Porter, Israel's brother; Joseph Hutchinson, an independent-minded farmer; Daniel Andrew, a well-to-do newcomer to the village; and Francis Nurse, Rebecca's husband and self-made successful farmer.

Most notable among the Putnam/Parris proponents were Edward Putnam, Thomas's brother; Jonathan Putnam, Thomas's cousin; Dr. William Griggs, Elizabeth Hubbard's great-uncle and guardian; Jonathan Walcott, Mary Walcott's uncle; and Nathaniel Ingersoll, keeper of the ordinary (tavern and restaurant) adjacent to Parris's parsonage, which became a central gathering place during the witch-hunts and the scene of numerous sightings and seizures involving the afflicted ones.

The sides were drawn early in Salem Village's unforgettable struggle with superstition, mass hysteria, and the forces of evil. And at the forefront of both contending factions stood a member of the Putnam family.

A Spreading Terror

On Sunday, April 3, Reverend Parris based his sermon on John 6:70: "Have not I chosen you twelve, and one of you is a devil." According to Puritan belief, church members are elected—that is, *chosen*—by God. The preacher's fiery offering propounded in several ways that there are no sinners so bad as church members (the *chosen*) who defect to the service of the devil. He described them as "sons and heirs of the devil, the free-holders of hell; whereas other sinners are but tenants." Since Rebecca Nurse and Martha Corey, two former members of the congregation, were imprisoned as alleged witches at the time, Parris's sermon implied their guilt before either had received a trial.

In midsermon, Sarah Towne Cloyce touched off a scandal when she rose from her seat and, in the words of Deodat Lawson, "to the amazement of the congregation" stormed out of the meetinghouse and slammed the door behind her.

After Sarah Cloyce had departed and reverberations of the slammed door settled, the Reverend Parris's next words gave further indication of his prejudgment. "Christ knows how many devils there are in his church and who they are."

A Puritan religious service. As powerful members of the community, ministers often used the pulpit to dictate behavior and to shame individual members.

Following the service, parishioners could speak of little else beyond the meaning of their parson's words and the significance of Cloyce's abrupt, if not altogether rude, exit. Her defenders maintained that she had suddenly been taken ill and that she had not meant to slam the door. An unexpected gust of wind, they said, had wrenched it from her feeble grasp. Cloyce's detractors thought otherwise, however, and attached a more ominous meaning to her actions. The truth, they knowingly declared, would be revealed in God's own good time.

Sarah Cloyce and Mary Towne Easty were sisters of the imprisoned Rebecca Nurse. As members of the Towne family of Topsfield, the sisters shared a history of feuding with the Putnam family over disputed land rights. Frances Hill explains:

> For years there had been enormous tension between the Putnams, together with some other Salem Villagers, and certain Topsfield inhabitants. The foundations of the conflict had been laid by the Massachusetts General Court when, in 1639, it gave Salem permission to expand in the direction of the Ipswich river and then, four years later, authorized some inhabitants of Ipswich to found a village in just the same area. The village later became Topsfield. As a result of these competing claims, quarrels about boundaries went on for centuries.

> One of the early settlers of this outlying area was John Putnam, the founding father of the clan, who was soon involved in bitter warfare over the ownership of the woodlands with three families: the Townes, Howes, and Eastys. Jacob Towne was the father of Rebecca Nurse and her sisters. Early on, he and John Howe cut down a tree that Putnam regarded as his, in front of his eyes. Soon afterward Putnam traveled forth with a band of nephews and sons to fell all the trees in the area. Two Towne men and two Easty men arrived to protest but were outnumbered. Putnam won that battle, but the war did not stop. It went on from one generation to another, in the style of a Sicilian blood feud, except that the blood

was not shed over time but conserved for the climax.

Hence, many of those accused of witchcraft in Salem Village
either had contested properties with the Putnams or had otherwise provoked their displeasure. Much as a compass arrow points
north, the fingers of the afflicted girls and women—including
both Ann Putnams—inevitably pointed at Sarah Cloyce.

A day or so after the Sabbath services, the afflicted girls gathered once again in the Parris parsonage and promptly entered into
a session of seizures. As a group, they envisioned Sarah standing
in a field in front of the house, in company with several witches.
They described a kind of devil's church and service in which they
saw Sarah partaking of the devil's sacrament of "red bread and
drink." They further claimed to see, in a scene visible only to
them, both Sarah Cloyce and Sarah Good serving as deacons.

Suddenly one of them shouted, "Oh, Goodwife Cloyce, I did
not think to see you here!" She spoke with feigned derision in a
grating tone that was becoming ever more familiar. "Is this a
time to receive the sacrament? You ran away on the Lord's day,
and scorned to receive it in the meetinghouse, and is this a time
to receive it? I wonder at you!"

Twice earlier, the girls had reported similar incidents of
witches' sacraments. The confessions of Tituba and Dorcas
Good had apparently stimulated the girls and the villagers into
thinking in terms of an organized society of witches, with its own
structure and rites, rather than of individual witches acting inde-
pendently. With the added aspect of conspiracy, the community
approached the next witch examination more determined than
ever to rid itself of the growing witch menace.

Jonathan Walcott and Nathaniel Ingersoll, energetic backers
of the Putnam/Parris faction, swore out a complaint against Sarah
Cloyce and Elizabeth Proctor on Monday, a warrant for their
arrest was issued on Friday, and they appeared before the magistrates on Monday, April 11. For the first time, however, the
hearings moved outside local limits and were held in Salem
Town. The witch-hunts were starting to spread terror throughout the colony.

FIERCE FITS

Occasionally, the afflicted girls reported seeing the specter of one of their own engaged in tormenting other afflicted persons. On April 11, 1692, Mary Warren, the house servant of John and Elizabeth Proctor, was accused by Abigail Williams of having signed the devil's book. Mary was examined by the magistrates eight days later. Judge John Hathorne conducted her examination:

HATHORNE: You were a little while ago an afflicted person. Now you are an afflicter. How comes this to pass?

WARREN: I look up to God and take it to be a great mercy of God.

H: What! Do you take it to be a great mercy to afflict others?

The usual assemblage of afflicted girls among the meetinghouse spectators had begun having fits as soon as Mary approached the court. The girls' hysteria, known to be communicable, apparently infected Mary (an earlier victim of fits), for she herself soon fell into convulsions. In *Records of Salem Witchcraft*, published in 1864, historian W. Elliot Woodward described the bizarre scene:

Shortly Mary Warren fell into a fit, and some of the afflicted cried out that she was going to confess, but Goody Corey and Proctor and his wife came in, in their apparition, and struck her down and said she should tell nothing.

Mary Warren continued a good space in a fit [so] that she did neither see, nor hear, nor speak. Afterwards she started up and said, "I will speak," and cried out "Oh! I am sorry for it, I am sorry for it," and wringed her hands, and fell a little while into a fit again, and then came to speak, but immediately her teeth were set. And then she fell into a violent fit and cried out, "Oh Lord help me! Oh good Lord save me!" And then afterwards cried again, "I will tell, I will tell," and then fell into a dead fit again. And afterwards cried, "I will tell! They did! They did! They did!" and then fell into a violent fit again. After a little recovery she cried, "I will tell! They brought me to it!" and then fell into a fit again, which fits continuing she was ordered to be had out.

Mary Warren was returned to prison. The magistrates had hoped that Mary would name the Proctors as the ones who "brought" her "to it," but she did not. After three weeks of further examinations and continuing fits in prison, she implicated both herself and John Proctor as tormentors. Her fits then became so fierce that her legs could not be uncrossed without breaking them.

"Her Spirit Is Gone to Prison"

As a sign of the colony's increased concern, several government dignitaries joined magistrates John Hathorne and Jonathan Corwin on the bench for Sarah Cloyce's hearing. Included in the group of six were such notable figures as Deputy Governor Thomas Danforth and Samuel Sewell, a minister noted for keeping a diary. The visiting officials, mostly from Boston, wanted to view the burgeoning witch situation firsthand.

Excited townspeople from Salem Village and throughout Essex County assembled in the meetinghouse located in the center of Salem Town on the corner of Washington and Main Streets, across from the expansive residence of John Hathorne. The change of location and the presence of visiting luminaries lent an air of celebrity to the proceedings. John Danforth himself presided over the hearing and questioned both the accused and the accusers.

If any of the local citizenry had expected Danforth and his colleagues to view the witchcraft accusations and the antics of

the afflicted ones with skepticism, they were soon disappointed. The visitors actually looked less critically upon the girls than their neighbors who had known them before their afflictions made them famous. Danforth, according to Frances Hill,

Minister Samuel Sewell joined the magistrates on the bench for Sarah Cloyce's hearing to determine if she was a witch. Sewell kept a diary.

was as firm a believer in the guilt of the accused as John
Hathorne [and] his line of inquiry differed from the magistrate's only in that it was directed as much at the
afflicted girls as at the accused witches. but this was
merely to establish the dreadful things done to them,
and by whom, not to probe their mental competence or
integrity. Those were never in question.

Danforth's presence elevated the hearings into a major event in
Massachusetts and escalated the witch-hunts with fatal consequences. His position as to the guilt of the accused witches armed
the girls and their confederates with greater authority to accelerate
their activities. The girls and their allies obliged, and the witch-
hunts roared forward, out of control, with a burst of new energy.

Danforth questioned John Indian, Mary Walcott, and Abigail
Williams. He asked each, in turn, who had hurt them. His manner suggested that he already knew the answers. John Indian
claimed Goody Proctor and Goody Cloyce as his tormentors.
And how had they hurt him? They had choked him, he
answered, and brought him the (devil's) book to sign.

At this point, Sarah Cloyce, unable to contain herself any
longer, shouted, "When did I hurt you?"

"A great many times," John Indian replied.

"Oh," Sarah said, "you are a grievous liar."

Danforth then turned to Abigail and asked her about the
gathering of witches at the Parris parsonage. "Abigail Williams!
did you see a company [gathering] at Mr. Parris's house?"

"Yes, sir, that was their sacrament."

"How many were there?"

"About forty, and Goody Cloyce and Goody Good were our
deacons."

Danforth next asked Mary Walcott if she had seen a "white
man," presumedly meaning Jesus Christ. She said that she had
and described him as "a fine grave man, and when he came, he
made all the witches tremble."

Author Frances Hill propounds the following explanation for
such sightings:

An unidentified woman is tried in court for practicing witchcraft. Although all of the accused in the Salem witch trials protested their innocence, the magistrates believed the antics of the young accusers.

These sights suggest longings in the girls' psyches that were the other side of the coin from the desire to torture and kill. They reveal yearnings for ecstasy and peace.

All the girls were on the verge of or well into adolescence. There were, in that time and place, no opportunities for sexual exploration outside marriage without whipping in this world and hellfire in the next. Even sexual yearnings were sinful, to be repressed into something more acceptable, such as visions of angels.

Unfortunately, for untold numbers of falsely accused witches, such yearnings were also repressed into something less acceptable.

As Sarah Cloyce's hearing neared its end, the girls did what they did best: They threw fits. And some of them cried out, "Oh, her spirit is gone to prison to her sister Nurse!"

The Price of Fame

Elizabeth Proctor's hearing commenced right after the tired body and being of Sarah Cloyce was led off to prison. Danforth first addressed Elizabeth, a tavern keeper and the pregnant wife of John Proctor, then her accusers:

Elizabeth Proctor, you understand whereof you are charged, viz., to be guilty of several acts of witchcraft; what say you to it? Speak the truth. And so you that are afflicted, you must speak the truth, as you will answer it before God another day. Mary Walcott, did this woman hurt you?

"I never saw her so as to be hurt by her," Mary answered. Danforth asked the same of Mercy Lewis, Ann Putnam, and Abigail Williams, but none could find words at that moment (apparently struck temporarily speechless). He next posed the same question to John Indian, who experienced no such speech impairment.

"This is the woman who came in her shift and choked me."
"Did she ever bring the book?" Danforth prompted.
"Yes sir."
"What to do?"
"To write."
"What, this woman?"
"Yes sir."
"Are you sure of it?"
"Yes sir."

Danforth again put the same question to Abigail Williams and Ann Putnam. Again, neither could answer. Turning to Elizabeth, he asked, "What do you say, Goody Proctor, to these things?"

"I take God in heaven to be my witness that I know nothing of it, no more that the child unborn." Her claim of innocence closely mimicked Rebecca Nurse's earlier sickbed plea.

When the girls' voices mysteriously returned, they accused Elizabeth of trying to coerce them into signing the devil's book. Abigail declared that Elizabeth had told them that her maid, Mary Warren, had already signed the book and demanded that Elizabeth acknowledge it. Elizabeth calmly replied, "Dear child, it is not so. There is another judgment, dear child."

Abigail reacted as she had so many times before, falling at once into a fit. Ann Putnam joined her immediately and together they cried out that they saw Goody Proctor's apparition perched on an overhead beam. Then they cried out on John Proctor as well, claiming that he was a wizard, whereupon, according to W. Elliot Woodward, "many, if not all of the bewitched had grievous fits." John Proctor's specter appeared to them next, tormenting Goodwives Pope and Bibber, who had recently joined the afflicted group.

Abigail shouted, "There is Goodman Proctor going to Mrs. Pope." Goodwife Pope fell instantly into a fit. "There is Goodman Proctor going to hurt Goody Bibber." And Goodwife Bibber was seized by convulsions.

Later that day both Proctors and Sarah Cloyce were sent to Boston jail, soon to be joined by Rebecca Nurse and Dorcas Good, who had been held in Salem prison. John and Elizabeth Proctor achieved later fame as the defendants in *The Crucible*, playwright Arthur Miller's fictionalized drama of the Salem witch trials. For this ill-starred pair, however, the price of fame came high.

Fault in High Places

The role of the afflicted girls (and others so bewitched, but principally the girls) became increasingly clear as more and more Salemites were accused and held over for trial. Irrespective of the original charges against them, most of the accused were jailed on grounds—spectral and otherwise—furnished by the afflicted girls during preliminary examinations.

Occasionally, one or more brave-hearted villagers refused to believe the girls' sightings and claims. One such denial occurred on March 28, during one of the many gatherings at Ingersoll's

As two of the accused Salem women face their judges, the afflicted girls cry out, pointing to unseen birds and claiming to be pinched and harmed by unknown forces under the control of the accused.

tavern. A young man named William Rayment, hoping for first-hand information, mentioned in the presence of several afflicted girls that he had heard Goody Proctor was to be examined the next day. Goody Ingersoll said she didn't think so, as she had heard nothing about it. One of the girls immediately cried out,

"There is Goody Proctor, there is Goody Proctor, old witch, I'll have her hang." Several girls joined in.

Before they could work themselves into their usual frenzy, Rayment told the first girl that he couldn't see a thing and didn't believe her. When Goody Ingersoll agreed and rebuked the girl for lying, the girls together tried to make a joke of it. Faced with such strong reproof, one of them dropped the pretense and said that she did it "for sport, they must have some sport."

While this revelation seems to suggest that the girls were not truly bewitched, which would invalidate all their claims, such incidents were rare and witnessed by only a few. Moreover, strong arguments have been made to support the premise that on most occasions the girls were not faking. Their more public claims and accompanying demonstrations, as in the courtroom, were completely believable. Historian Chadwick Hansen writes:

> Indeed, these courtroom fits were so convincing that most of the indictments were for witchcraft committed during the preliminary examination rather than for the offenses named in the original complaint. The typical order of events in the Salem witchcraft cases was: (1) the swearing out of a complaint for acts of witchcraft; (2) a preliminary examination during which the afflicted persons had convulsive fits; (3) an indictment for acts of witchcraft performed during the preliminary examination; and (4) the trial.
>
> The direct cause of these fits, in the courtroom or out of it, was, of course, not witchcraft itself, but the afflicted person's fear of witchcraft. If fits were occasioned by fear of someone like Bridget Bishop, who was actually practicing witchcraft [see chapter five], they might also be occasioned by fear of someone who was only suspected of practicing it.

It seems certain that the girls, although not *really* threatened by witchcraft, truly *felt* endangered by it. And just as certainly, their fear led to a host of false accusations.

But the girls do not alone bear the blame for the tragedies resulting from their untrue allegations. They had sufficient help from their elders and the court officials—most of whom accepted the girls' wildest claims as fact without hesitation—to establish at least equal fault in higher places.

A Torrent of Accusations

On May 10, while examining George Jacobs Sr., a seventy-year-old grandfather who walked with two sticks, magistrate John Hathorne established a second critical precedent for future trials (the admission of spectral evidence being the first). Jacobs, when accused of witchery by Sarah Churchill, his twenty-year-old servant girl, declared, "The devil can go in any shape . . . can take any likeness." After due consideration, Hathorne responded.

This depiction of the trial of seventy-year-old grandfather George Jacobs Sr. re-creates the tumult and hysteria that must have dominated the scene.

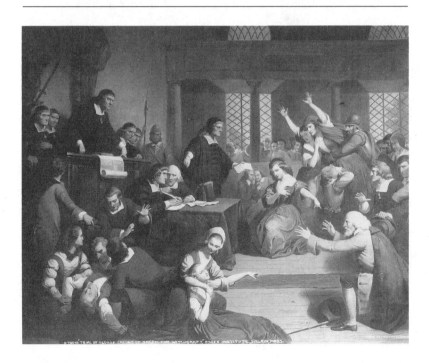

"Not without their consent," he said. Although Hathorne's pronouncement had no firm authority, all of the magistrates and judges in subsequent hearings and trials supported his opinion, apparently out of a sense that it *ought* to be true. With these four words, Hathorne rejected the strongest argument against the use of spectral evidence.

Hathorne's assertion meant, in effect, that anyone capable of projecting his or her spectral image (of which most defendants were accused) must be willingly in league with the devil and, by extension, a witch. In other words, *the devil cannot assume the shape of an innocent person.* The general acceptance of Hathorne's ruling released a torrent of accusations, resulting in the arrest of at least thirty-nine more suspects in May.

A New Charter

On May 14, Sir William Phipps, the new governor of Massachusetts Bay Colony, and Increase Mather, the esteemed clergyman, arrived from England. With them, they brought a new provincial charter for the colony—and a glimmer of hope for the accused.

Chapter 5

The Court of Oyer
and Terminer

As the calendar arrived at June, the fields of Essex County lay unattended at a critical time, and a pervasive fear smothered the life's breath of Salem Village and surrounding communities. The life-choking tide of witch accusations had swirled outward from the town and village of Salem and thrashed like an angry surf upon the countryside. The ranks of indicted witches had by then swelled to include representatives from Gloucester, Beverly, Lynn, Malden, Amesbury, Billerica, Marblehead, Boston, Charleston, and Andover. Goodmen and goodwives trusted no one—not neighbor, friend, or relative, not even each other—lest they be hauled in to answer someone's soul-condemning allegation. Good people everywhere looked to the forthcoming witch trials with the same fears, but with a growing hope that the trials would hold back the surging sea of accusations and deliver them from evil.

In Name Only

On June 2, 1692, new governor Sir William Phipps appointed a special Court of Oyer and Terminer to try the accused witches. (*Oyer and terminer* is an Anglo-French phrase meaning "to hear and determine.") The original court comprised seven judges, only one of whom, Bartholomew Gedney, resided locally. Of the remaining jurists, Samuel Sewell, John Richards, William Sergeant, and Wait Winthrop hailed from Boston, Nathaniel

Saltonstall came from Haverhill, and the chief judge and new deputy governor, William Stoughton, lived in Dorchester. This court represented a group of widely experienced magistrates, as far removed from the spiteful accusations and witch hearings as was possible to assemble. But they did not necessarily come to the trials without personal bias and preconceived opinions. Three of them—Gedney, Stoughton, and Sewell—had already taken some small part in the hearings.

The trials commenced immediately. To call them trials tends to strain credulity, as, in truth, they were but a replication of the evidence and testimonies presented at the earlier hearings. Court records of the original examinations were admitted at trial and accepted as proven facts by the new magistrates. The only new evidence was such as could be collected in the interval between hearing and trial. Little or none of the new evidence favored the accused, who were condemned without benefit of a defense. (In early Puritan New England, God was presumed to take care of the innocent.) For each defendant, the hearing constituted the trial in all but name.

A Solitary Figure

Bridget Bishop suffered the unenviable distinction of becoming the first accused witch to be tried. Bridget, a tavern keeper, was the widow of Thomas Oliver and the then present wife of Salem sawyer (one who saws timber) Edward Bishop. A matron well into her sixties, or perhaps even seventies, Bridget's history of having once been accused, tried, and apparently acquitted of witchcraft in 1679–80 worked against her the second time around.

Cotton Mather described her trial with childlike candor, remarking that "there was little occasion to prove the witchcraft, this being evident and notorious to all beholders."

The afflicted girls accused her of murdering several young children. Elizabeth Balch, an acquaintance of the Bishops, testified that she had witnessed an argument between the couple, after which Edward Bishop told her that Bridget was a "bad wife"; and that "the devil had come bodily to her . . . and she sat up all night with the devil."

Several local men claimed that Bridget's specter had hovered over them. And two other men testified that

> being employed by Bridget Bishop, alias Oliver, of Salem to help take down the cellar wall of the old house she formerly lived in, we the said deponents [evidence givers], in holes in the old wall belonging to the said cellar, found several puppets made up of rags and hogs' bristles with headless pins in them with the points outward.

A doll with pins in it—the classic charm of black magic—was, and is still, often buried within walls by witches. Evidence of such has been discovered hidden within cottage walls in twentieth-century England. In seventeenth-century New England, such a find was devastatingly incriminating to an owner accused of witchery. When questioned about the dolls, Bridget, according to Cotton Mather, could not offer an accounting for them to the court "that was reasonable or tolerable."

Little is known of Bridget's actual testimony at trial, such records either having been not kept or lost in time. But the foregoing claims against her combined to form a body of evidence more than sufficient in the minds of the court to convict her. The court reached a quick verdict of guilty and sentenced Bridget Bishop to death. Their judgment posed an immediate problem, however, since no provisions for the death penalty in witch cases then existed under Massachusetts law. The problem went away

A facsimile of Bridget Bishop's death warrant signed by the sheriff. Bishop was the first woman to be convicted of witchcraft in Salem.

Bridget Bishop is hanged from a limb of an oak on Gallows Hill as onlookers jeer and condemn her.

on June 8, when the General Court reinstated an old colonial law that proclaimed witchcraft a capital offense punishable by death.

On June 10, High Sheriff George Corwin escorted Bridget Bishop to the summit of Gallows Hill and hanged her solitary figure from the limb of a great oak tree. She became the first of nineteen accused witches to be so executed in Salem Town in 1692.

A Rejection of Spectral Evidence

Shortly after Bridget's hanging, one of the magistrates, Nathaniel Saltonstall of Haverhill, resigned from the court. In a letter to a friend, Saltonstall explained that he was "very much dissatisfied with the proceedings of it." Although he refused to publicly criticize the court's conduct, he could never bring himself to believe the courtroom demonstrations of the afflicted girls

Royal governor of Massachusetts William Phipps wrote to several prominent Puritan ministers asking for confirmation of the acceptance of spectral evidence.

or the evidence upon which convictions were won. He is said to have taken to strong drink out of his sense of powerlessness to alter the course of the witch proceedings. Magistrate Jonathan Corwin replaced Saltonstall when the trials resumed on June 28.

During a lull after the first trial, Sir William Phipps, concerned over stirrings of dissent as to the validity of spectral evidence, wrote to the ministers of Boston for their opinion. In the wake of Bridget Bishop's hanging, he considered the matter of witchcraft to hold strong religious as well as legal implications. A group of twelve Puritan ministers, including Increase and Cotton Mather, sent a reply to Phipps's plea for guidance on June 15. They urged caution, but they also recommended continuing a swift and lively legal action against witches.

The text of the ministers' response, entitled "Return of the Several Ministers Consulted," and believed to have been authored by Cotton Mather, states in part:

> We judge that in the prosecution of these, and all such witchcrafts, there is need of a very critical and exquisite caution, lest by too much credulity for things received only upon the Devil's authority there be a door opened for a long train of miserable consequences, and Satan get an advantage over us, for we should not be ignorant of his devices. . . .
>
> Nevertheless, we cannot but humbly recommend unto the government the speedy and vigorous prosecution of

such as have rendered themselves obnoxious [suspected witches], according to the directions given in the Laws of God and the wholesome statutes of the English nation for the detection of witchcraft.

In essence, this document rejected the use of spectral evidence, the primary evidence against the accused witches. And it called for disallowing the testimony of confessed witches (which might have been derived only after coercion and therefore unreliable). Moreover, it warned against noisy and disorderly hearings, such as shouted accusations and other unsolicited outbursts in the courtroom. Finally, it suggested that the rejection of spectral evidence and the testimony of confessed witches might "put a period" to the affair, including accusations.

A Renewed Commitment

Meanwhile, the arrests and examinations continued. A major difference of opinion between the magistrates and the ministers then developed. The ministers pointedly recommended that the magistrates try discrediting all "things received only upon the Devil's authority"—that is, spectral evidence and the confessions of witches. But more than a recommendation was needed to halt the rush to judgment, as Frances Hill observes:

Unless the ministers followed up their strictures about the need for caution and set aside their recommendations for vigor and speed, it was inevitable that juries would continue to convict accused witches and that judges would continue to sentence them to death. They would do so on the evidence that had damned the accused at their examinations, that is, the afflicted girls' tortures. The *Return* would not impede the course of events but encourage it.

The ministers wanted to voice their misgivings without opposing the judges. If they had been wholehearted about the unreliability of spectral evidence, they would have suggested barring the girls from the courtroom.

Then the cases against most of the accused witches would have collapsed and the trials would have ceased. But the ministers chose to be swept along by a dangerous tide instead of trying to stem it.

After a two-week debate between the magistrates and the ministers during which they failed to reach agreement, the trials resumed on June 30.

At that session, and at two later sessions on August 5 and September 9, the judges showed no signs of judicial dissent. They could not speedily and vigorously prosecute the accused without continuing the methods already used so effectively. To a judge, they renewed their commitment to the use of spectral evidence.

A Wrongful Interpretation

Five people faced the court on June 30: Sarah Good, Rebecca Nurse, Susannah Martin, Elizabeth Howe, and Sarah Wildes. In those trials, the afflicted girls and young women surpassed even their earlier sovereign performances, flinging themselves into fits immediately upon the appearance in court of the defendants. And the details of their tortured exhibitions at the preliminary hearings were then summarily entered into evidence.

The most important trial of this session was not that of Sarah Good, the first suspected witch to be indicted, but that of Rebecca Nurse. Earlier, of course, John Hathorne's sister and brother-in-law had testified for Rebecca at her preliminary hearing. Hathorne himself had experienced some misgivings about Rebecca's guilt while examining her.

Later, while Rebecca had awaited trial—shackled, cold, and damp in Salem prison—thirty-nine of her neighbors had signed a petition in her behalf. The petition stated that according to their observation "her life and conversation were according to her profession [as a Christian], and we never had any cause or grounds to suspect her of any such thing as she is now accused of." Even Jonathan Putnam, who had with Edward Putnam sworn out the original complaint against her, signed the petition after experiencing an apparent change of heart. Nor could the jury

PRINCIPAL EVIDENCE AND NEW TORMENTS

Shortly after the jury reconsidered Rebecca Nurse's acquittal and subsequently returned a guilty verdict, her relatives did everything they could in an attempt to right what must have seemed to them a terrible wrong. They began by requesting an explanatory statement of the jury's decision from jury foreman Thomas Fisk. Fisk replied:

> July 4, 1692. I, Thomas Fisk, the subscriber [writer] hereof, being one of them that were of the jury the last week at Salem court upon the trial of Rebecca Nurse, etc., being desired by some of the relations to give a reason why the jury brought her in guilty after her verdict [of] not guilty, I do hereby give my reasons to be as follows, *viz.*
>
> When the verdict not guilty was [brought in] the honored Court was pleased to object against it, saying to them that they think they let slip the words which the prisoner at the bar spoke against herself, which were spoken in reply to Goodwife Hobbes and her daughter, who had been faulty in setting their hands to the Devil's Book as they have confessed formerly. The words were, "What, do these persons give in evidence against me now? They used to come among us." After the honored Court had manifested their dissatisfaction of the verdict several of the jury declared themselves desirous to go out again, and thereupon the honored Court gave leave. But when we came to consider of the case I could not tell how to take her words as an evidence against her till she had a further opportunity to put her sense upon them, if she would take it. And then, going into court, I mentioned the words aforesaid, which by one of the Court were affirmed to have been spoken by her, she being then at the bar, but made no reply nor interpretation of them, whereupon these words were to me a principal evidence against her.
>
> *Thomas Fisk*

Upon receipt of Fisk's statement, Rebecca Nurse issued a statement of her own, explaining her reason for not responding to Fisk. Because of deafness she had not heard Fisk over the courtroom din. Governor Sir William Phipps granted Rebecca a reprieve on the basis of these documents. But when the afflicted ones complained of new torments shortly thereafter, Phipps rescinded his reprieve. Rebecca Nurse was hanged on Gallows Hill on July 19, 1692.

believe Rebecca to be a witch. They returned a verdict of not guilty. Robert Calef wrote that when jury foreman Thomas Fisk announced their verdict "immediately all the accusers in the court, and suddenly after all the afflicted outside out of court, made an hideous outcry, to the amazement not only of the spectators but the court also." Some historians suggest that their "hideous outcry" may have been more planned than spontaneous. In light of so many previous outcries, it must have been spectacular indeed to amaze spectators and judges alike. In either case, such an out-

When Rebecca Nurse was found innocent of the charges against her, Chief Justice William Stoughton was instrumental in having the verdict changed to guilty.

burst implies their genuine fear that a witch might be acquitted.

The verdict apparently upset the judges as much as the spectators. "One of the judges expressed himself not satisfied," wrote Calef. "Another of them, as he was going off the bench, said they would have her indicted anew."

Chief Justice William Stoughton, according to Calef, "said he would not impose upon the jury," but asked them if they had thought about the possible implications of something Rebecca had said earlier:

When one [Deliverance] Hobbes, who had confessed herself a witch, was brought into court to witness against her, the prisoner turning her head to her said, "What, do you bring her? She is one of us," or [words] to that effect.

Stoughton suggested to the jury that Rebecca meant "one of us witches." When foreman Fisk asked her what she meant, Rebecca did not answer. He took her silence to mean her tacit agreement with Stoughton's interpretation. The jury then deliberated again, this time returning with a guilty verdict.

Hell in the Hereafter

In a statement taken by her relatives after the new verdict came in, Rebecca explained her silence:

> These presents do humbly show to the honored court and jury that, I being informed that the jury brought me in guilty upon my saying that Goodwife Hobbes and her daughter [Abigail] were of our company, but I intended no otherways than as they were prisoners with us, therefore did then, and yet do, judge them not legal evidence against their fellow prisoners. And I being something hard of hearing, and full of grief, none informing me of how the court took up my words, and therefore had not opportunity to declare what I intended when I said they were of our company.

In other words, Rebecca had not answered Fisk because she had not heard him, owing to her deafness and emotional upset. By saying "one of us," she had meant *prisoners* not witches and questioned the legality of prisoners's testifying against her. Her statement availed her nothing. The guilty verdict stood.

Although the court then sentenced her to death, all was not yet lost. Rebecca's friends succeeded in securing her reprieve from Governor Sir William Phipps. Once Phipps had granted the reprieve, however, the afflicted girls immediately "renewed their dismal outcries against her," wrote Calef. And at the urging of "some Salem gentleman"—probably Nicholas Noyes, an obese, zealous Salem pastor—Phipps rescinded his reprieve.

Following this unkind reversal of fortune, Rebecca's already wretched luck grew worse. The members of her church in Salem Town voted unanimously to excommunicate her. The church record shows:

> 1692, July 3. After sacrament the elders [John Higginson and Nicholas Noyes] propounded to the church—and it

was by unanimous vote consented to—that our sister Nurse, being a convicted witch by the court and condemned to die, should be excommunicated, which was accordingly done in the afternoon, she being present.

To a devoutly Christian Puritan woman, excommunication from the church meant certain damnation. The fragile, seventy-one-year-old Rebecca Nurse faced not only death but hell in the hereafter.

Of the remaining four defendants tried on June 30, not one escaped the hangman's rope. Sarah Good's fate, like so many others, had been almost certainly determined during her preliminary hearing. Nothing happened at her trial to dissuade the minds of magistrates bent on achieving convictions.

An accused witch awaits trial, reading the Bible by candlelight.

A Witty Witch

Susannah Martin, who by her own admission had established herself as a witch in Amesbury in 1669, defended herself in a manner unlike someone fighting for her life. At her hearing in May, she had faced her accusers and their customary demonstrations with twinkling eyes and a laugh that shocked the solemnity of the court. When the magistrates admonished her she said, "Well may I laugh at such folly."

"What do you think ails them," the magistrates asked.

"I don't desire to spend my judgment on it."

"Don't you think they are bewitched?"

"No, I do not think they are! If they be dealing with the black arts, you may know as well as I." Responding to testimony about her spectral misdeeds, she implied that the specters might be the devil in disguise. "He that appeared in the shape of Samuel, a glorified saint, may appear in anyone's shape." Her reference to the biblical witch of Endor was the second time such suggestion of Satan as specter had been voiced in court.

The magistrates chose not to match wits with the irreverent witch from Amesbury. The jury eventually convicted her largely on the basis of testimony of her witchcraft volunteered by her neighbors. The court condemned her to hang.

A Wonderful Daughter-in-Law

Elizabeth Howe also fell victim to the complaints of angry neighbors. She and James Howe, her blind husband of thirty-four years, and two daughters lived on the disputed Topsfield-Ipswich border. Both townships claimed the right to tax residents along the boundary line, where arguments over property rights flared up routinely. Elizabeth, an intelligent woman of fine character, belonged by birth and marriage to families that frequently opposed the Putnams in land disputes. Not surprisingly, Ann Putnam, Mercy Lewis, and Mary Walcott targeted her as one of their tormentors and accused her of pinching and sticking pins in them.

When arrested on May 29, Elizabeth denied even knowing the girls and said, "If it was the last moment I was to live, God knows I am innocent of anything in this nature."

Quarrelsome neighbors spoke against Elizabeth at her trial. The testimony of Samuel Perley was particularly hurtful:

> We having a daughter about ten years of age being in a sorrowful condition, *this being soon after a falling out that had been between James Howe and his wife and myself* [italics added to emphasize what was possibly the *real* reason for Perley's charges], our daughter told us that it was James Howe's wife that afflicted her both night and day sometimes complaining of being pricked with pins and sometimes falling down in dreadful fits. . . . One day we went to several doctors and they told us that Hannah [their daughter] was under an evil hand. Our daughter told us that when she came near the fire or water this witch pulls me in.

Timothy and Deborah Perley, Hannah's uncle and aunt, filled in further details of the girl's supposed torment. They quoted Hannah as screaming, "There's that woman. She goes into the oven and out again." Deborah Perley added that young Hannah "fell into a dreadful fit, and when I have asked her when she said 'that woman' what woman she meant, she told me James Howe's wife."

In Elizabeth's favor, the Reverend Samuel Phillips, a Topsfield minister, testified about visiting Hannah shortly after she had emerged from a fit outside her house in Elizabeth's presence. He said that Elizabeth took the girl by the hand and said, "Did I hurt you?" The girl said, "No, never, and if I did complain of you in my fits I know not that I did so." At that point, Phillips said, the girl's brother called out from a nearby window. "Say Goodwife Howe is a witch, say she is a witch." The minister then added his own assessment.

"No wonder that the child in her fits did mention Goodwife Howe," he said, "when her nearest relations were so frequent in expressing their suspicions in the child's hearing . . . that the said Goodwife Howe, was an instrument of mischief to the child."

Elizabeth, described by her ninety-four-year-old father-in-law as a wonderful daughter-in-law "loving, obedient, and kind" to her blind husband, "tenderly leading him about by the hand," would be missed by her family. Irrespective of such moving testimony, Elizabeth Howe was adjudged guilty and sentenced to hang.

Eliminating the Witch Problem

Sarah Wildes, wife of farmer John Wildes, also resided in the contentious town of Topsfield. She is said to have been very protective of family property, never lending farm implements and forbidding neighborly trespass without express permission. Little else is known of her, except that she, too, was pronounced guilty and sentenced to hang.

The Court of Oyer and Terminer, it seems, intended to use all means at its disposal to eliminate the witch problem within its jurisdiction.

Chapter 6

Gallows Hill

ON JULY 19, 1692, Sarah Good, Rebecca Nurse, Susannah Martin, Elizabeth Howe, and Sarah Wildes were hanged. The execution site has never been ascertained for sure, but tradition and logic maintain that the witch hangings took place on Gallows Hill, also known as Witch Hill.

Coarse Approval

Gallows Hill is the first good-sized hill on the only overland route out of Salem. It is reached by taking Boston Road northward from Essex Street. Water lies in all other directions. The

The view from the lookout on Witch Hill. This was the last sight of home for many of the accused witches.

*A convicted witch is led off to her execution as the crowd taunts and jeers her
along the way.*

condemned witches were carried by cart down Essex Street for
three-quarters of a mile, then north on Boston Road, past fields
and orchards on the right and the North River and marshlands
on the left.

At the foot of Gallows Hill, the cart began a sharp upward
climb, carrying its condemned passengers as close to the place of
their execution as possible, until the steep, rocky ascent denied
the cart farther passage. Those who were about to die were made
to walk the rest of the way to their final destination in life—a
huge spreading oak or locust tree on the summit. From there, in
life's last moments, their eyes could scan the sea and sky, and the
fields and forests of the world they were so soon to leave.

Along the path of their ultimate journey, the condemned
ones suffered a merciless onslaught of taunts and jeers from the
afflicted girls and a huge crowd that followed alongside the cart.

Some of the cart's doomed passengers, still in chains, sat huddled on the floor with head and arms on knees. Some stood resolutely erect. A few wept, some prayed, and still others appeared lost in thought, perhaps envisioning an afterlife of everlasting hellfire, such as their Puritan religion would surely lead them to expect. Those too weak to walk the final yards to the hanging tree could count on the willing assistance of marshals and constables.

If any of the condemned ones did indeed entertain visions of a grim afterlife, their last moments must have yielded even further torment to those who contemplated the means by which they would get from this life to the next. Hanging—a method of execution handed down to the Puritans by the English—is, at best, a most unpleasant way to die.

A graphic account of a hanging handed down in English folklore describes a woman at the moment of dropping: "She gave a faint scream, and, for two or three minutes after she was suspended, appeared to be in great agony, moving her hands up and down frequently."

In 1774 Dr. Alexander Munro, professor of anatomy at Edinburgh, told James Boswell that "a man is suffocated by hanging in a rope just as by having his respiration stopped by having a pillow pressed on his face. . . . For some time after a man is thrown over he is sensible and is conscious that he is *hanging*."

Almost a century later, an English textbook described the anatomical effects of hanging as

> lividity and swelling of the face, especially of the ears and lips, which appear distorted: the eyelids swollen, and of a bluish color; the eyes red, projecting forward, and sometimes projecting out of their cavities . . . a bloody froth or frothy mucus sometimes escaping from the lips or nostrils . . . the fingers are generally much contracted or firmly clenched . . . the urine or feces are sometimes involuntarily expelled at the moment of death.

Those condemned to hang on Gallows Hill suffered similar experiences. And while the bodies of the doomed jerked convulsively at rope's end, the afflicted girls and the frenzied crowd

After the hanging, the bodies of many victims were disposed of without a proper burial.

jeered in coarse approval until the last suspended figure could no longer hear.

A Grave Digger's Wages

While Sarah Good awaited the hangman's hood and noose, the bullying Nicholas Noyes told her that she was a witch and knew it. He called on her to confess. Her reply is legend. "You are a liar," she snarled. "I am no more a witch than you are a wizard, and if you take away my life God will give you blood to drink." Her reply shocked the crowd assembled on the hill, for they were not the words expected of a seventeenth-century Christian.

Oddly, twenty-five years later, Noyes, according to Salem lore, choked on his own blood while he lay dying. Salemites remembered Sarah Good's words with a chill. Nathaniel Hawthorne would later adapt the incident for his *House of the Seven Gables.*

It is not known in what order the five women climbed the ladder leaning against the tree's great limb and stepped off into whatever fate awaited them. But witnesses to their end remarked that all departed with dignity. In light of what is known about Sarah Good's exit, it might be inferred that some left more quietly than others. Speculation suggests that the more docile members of the group went first, perhaps led by the devout Rebecca Nurse, and possibly followed by the Christian Elizabeth Howe, and next by the gentle Sarah Wildes. Susannah Martin's exit might have rivaled Sarah Good's for eleventh-hour impudence.

Once dead, the bodies of all five women were cut down from the tree and callously disposed of in shallow graves in a crevice on Gallows Hill. The thrifty Puritans were not inclined to waste money on a grave digger's wages.

A Lingering Doubt

The next session of trials began on August 5. George Burroughs, John and Elizabeth Proctor, George Jacobs Sr., John Willard, and Martha Carrier stood before the court and their accusers and were all found guilty and sentenced to hang. Elizabeth Proctor was spared because of her pregnancy. The others were hanged on August 19. All are said to have died well.

According to Thomas Brattle, a Salem merchant, Proctor, Willard, and Burroughs made particularly strong impressions as they went to their deaths. As Brattle later wrote:

> In the opinion of many unprejudiced, considerate, and considerable spectators, some of the condemned went out of the world not only with as great protestation but also as good shows of innocency as men could do.
>
> They protested their innocency as in the presence of the great God whom forthwith they were to appear before. They wished, and declared their wish, that their blood might be the last innocent blood shed upon that account. . . . They . . . seemed to be very sincere, upright, and sensible of their circumstances on all accounts, especially Proctor and Willard, whose whole management of themselves from the jail to the gallows and whilst at the gallows was very affecting and melting to the hearts of some considerable spectators.

Boston merchant Robert Calef provided the most thorough account of George Burroughs's final moments:

> Mr. Burroughs was carried in a cart with the others through the streets of Salem to execution. When he was upon the ladder he made a speech for the clearing of his innocency, with such solemn and serious expressions as

A HUMBLE PETITION

Once accused of witchcraft, Mary Towne Easty, the fifty-seven-year-old wife of Isaac Easty and mother of seven children, stood little chance of escaping conviction. Ann Putnam Sr., wife of the powerful Thomas Putnam, lodged the first charge against Mary, calling her a witch who was the daughter of a witch—along with Mary's sisters Rebecca Towne Nurse and Sarah Towne Cloyce. To add to Mary's vulnerability, Rebecca Nurse had already been hanged on similar charges. Also to Mary's detriment, her family was involved in the ongoing Topsfield land disputes with the Putnam family. Her chances of acquittal numbered few and none.

Mary Easty was sentenced to death on September 9, 1692. She accepted her fate with calm resignation. After her sentencing and after saying her last farewells to her family, Mary addressed the court and the governor with a petition so eloquent and keenly distressing as to evoke tears from almost all present:

> Your poor and humble petitioner knowing my own innocence (blessed be the Lord for it) . . . and seeing clearly the wiles and subtlety of my accusers . . . I petition to your honors not for my own life, for I know I must die and my appointed time is set [September 22]. But the Lord he knows that if it be possible no more innocent blood may be shed, which undoubtedly cannot be avoided in the way and course you go in. I question not but your honors does to the utmost of your power in the discovery and selection of witchcraft and witches, and would not be guilty of innocent blood for the world. But by my own innocence I know you are in the wrong way. The Lord in his infinite mercy direct you in this great work. If it be his blessed will that no more innocent blood be shed I would humbly beg of you that your honors would be pleased to examine these afflicted persons strictly and keep them apart some time, and likewise to try some of these confessing witches, I being confident there is several of them has belied themselves and others, as will appear if not in this world, I am sure in the world to come whither I am now going. And I question not but you'll see an alteration of these things they myself and others having made a league with the Devil we cannot confess. I know and the Lord knows, as will shortly appear, they belie me and so I question not but they do others. . . . The Lord knows that . . . I know not the least thing of witchcraft, therefore I cannot, I dare not belie my own soul. I beg your honors not to deny this my humble petition from a poor dying innocent person, and I question not but the Lord will give a blessing to your endeavors.

Mary Easty died without knowing that her fifty-year-old younger sister, Sarah Cloyce, never came to trial. Sarah was reprieved at the end of the witch-hunts.

were to the admiration of all present. His prayer (which
he concluded by repeating the Lord's Prayer) was so well
worded, and uttered with such composedness, and such
(at least seeming) fervency of spirit as was very affecting
and drew tears from many (so that it seemed to some
that the spectators would hinder the execution).

Burroughs, himself a minister, startled the gathering by reciting
the Lord's Prayer flawlessly. A popular belief of the day held that
witches could not repeat the prayer properly. This belief, in turn,
stemmed from the notion that witches recite the Lord's Prayer
backward at their sabbats (midnight gatherings). True or not,
Burroughs's recitation left a lingering doubt about his guilt in the
collective Salem conscience.

Smoke from the Hangman's Pipe

John Proctor, who had been arrested a week before Bridget
Bishop, the first accused witch to be hanged, was himself sentenced to hang for little more than coming unsummoned to his
wife's defense. His unexpected intrusion at court sparked a com-
motion, and he had to shout to be heard. Abigail Williams seized
the opportunity to cast suspicion on Elizabeth's gruff and out-
spoken—but until then unaccused—husband. Over the tumult,
Abigail shouted, "Why he can pinch as well as she!"

The magistrates, who relied on the words and reactions of
the girls as their principal source of truth, apparently heard her
voice and not John Proctor's. Records of Elizabeth's hearing fail
to show what John said in her defense. Whatever he said either
went unheard or was deemed irrelevant by the court. Worse,
John's unscheduled appearance availed his wife little and
resulted in his own indictment. One of the magistrates answered
John's arguments only with a reproof:

> You see, the devil will deceive you. The children could
> see what you was [*sic*] going to do before the woman was
> hurt [a reference to Gertrude Pope, supposedly assailed
> by Proctor's specter]. I would advise you to repentance,
> for the devil is bringing you out.

Whether John repented at the end will never be known. At his hanging, when he attempted to speak, he choked on smoke from the pipe of the hangman, an inveterate smoker. John Proctor's last words went unspoken.

Elizabeth Proctor was allowed, in the idiom of the time, to "plead her belly." Her hanging was postponed until the birth of her baby but was later rescinded. John's estate was confiscated and proceeds from it were used to pay for the couple's jail costs. Elizabeth and the eleven children of her late, prolific husband lived out their lives in abject poverty.

Options

The court convicted the lame, white-haired, and toothless George Jacobs Sr. in part on the testimony of his granddaughter Margaret Jacobs. She had admitted earlier that Jacobs practiced witchcraft and was herself imprisoned for her confession. Her later retraction did not help her grandfather, nor did he help himself. Facing the magistrates, he disagreeably proclaimed his innocence. "You tax me for a wizard; you may as well tax me buzzard. I have done no harm."

A judge then asked him to recite the Lord's Prayer, a standard witch test, and Jacobs stumbled fatally while voicing it. Frustrated by his failure, he shouted defiantly at the court, "Well burn me or hang me! I'll stand in the truth of Christ. I know nothing of it." ("It" referred to the charges of witchcraft lodged against him.) The court opted to hang him.

Dead and Moldering

A dispirited and disgusted Martha Carrier cried out to the judges, "It is a shameful thing that you should mind these folks that are out of their minds." She then faced the afflicted girls and said, "You lie! I am wronged! . . . The devil is a liar!" Martha protested her innocence to the very end, which surprised Cotton Mather, who felt nothing but contempt for her. In his quickly drafted history of the Salem proceedings published in late 1692, he wrote: "The rampant hag was the person of whom the confessions of the witches, and of her own children among the rest, agreed that the Devil had promised her that she should be queen of Hell." Martha Carrier was condemned to death largely on the testimony of her own children. One old record of the Salem witch outbreak states that her sons Richard and Andrew confessed to being witches only after they were "tied . . . neck and heels till the blood was ready to come out of their noses." The use of torture as an instrument for eliciting confessions was not uncommon. During the Salem witch-hunts, writes author and journalist Frances Hill,

> well over a hundred [alleged witches] languished for months in cramped, dark, stinking prisons, hungry and thirsty, never moving from the walls they were chained to, unsure if they would ever go free. Some were tortured by the strange method known as "tying neck and heels," their bodies forced into hoops, necks roped to feet. Others were made to stand without rest during interminable sessions of questioning. Many were even more exquisitely tortured by knowing that their children were left unprovided for when they were seized. Mothers wondered if their babies still lived.

In the case of Richard and Andrew Carrier, when it later became clear that their own lives were no longer endangered, they retracted their confessions. By then, Martha Carrier's body lay dead and moldering in a shallow, rocky grave.

Executions and Reprieves

The final sessions started on September 9. Another six alleged witches were tried, convicted, and sentenced to death: Martha Corey, Mary Easty, Alice Parker, Ann Pudeator, Dorcas Hoar, and Mary Bradbury. Eight days later, the court delivered death sentences to nine more defendants: Margaret Scott, Wilmot Redd, Samuel Wardwell, Mary Parker, Abigail Falkner, Rebecca Eames, Mary Lacy, Ann Foster, and Abigail Hobbes. The last five were spared, Abigail Falkner because of pregnancy, the rest through confessions of guilt. A tenth defendant, Giles Corey, an irascible eighty-year-old farmer, contested the court's right to try him. Because Corey refused to plead his innocence or guilt, the court, under existing law, ordered that weights be piled upon his body until he either entered a plea or died. Corey chose to die.

On September 19, in an open field beside Salem jail, Corey was pressed to death under the weight of many stones. According to tradition, the defiant farmer went to his death uttering only an occasional gasping request for "more weight."

Three days hence, on September 22, eight more condemned witches were hanged: Martha Corey, Mary Easty, Alice Parker, Mary Parker, Ann Pudeator, Margaret Scott, Wilmot Redd, and Samuel Wardwell. These were the last hangings in Salem Town.

Yet the witch-hunt continued in October. As the fame of the afflicted girls spread, neighboring towns sought their help. More than fifty people were accused in Andover, with many confessing to being witches. Gloucester imprisoned four women on witch charges. But the credibility of the afflicted girls peaked and started to wane as their accusations became increasingly numerous and outrageous. They began to overstep the bounds of believability by accusing several prominent and powerful people of witchery, including the wives of Governor Phipps and Increase Mather. The citizenry began to look upon the girls as

The famous last words of Giles Corey reverberate through history and give strength to all those who protest their innocence. Asked to proclaim his guilt as his accusers piled heavy rocks on his chest, Corey refused, murmuring the words, "More weight."

possessed rather than bewitched, that is, as agents—rather than victims—of the devil.

On October 3, Increase Mather—president of Harvard and Boston's leading minister and politician—delivered a sermon called "Cases of Conscience Concerning Evil Spirits Personating Men." His sermon, later published as an essay, cast grave doubt on the validity of spectral evidence—the girls' visions. In it, Mather stated: "It were better that ten suspected witches should escape, than that one innocent person should be condemned." Mather brought the full weight of his moral authority and political position to bear against the continued use of spectral evidence to obtain convictions.

On October 12, Governor Sir William Phipps ordered a moratorium on all witch trials. Two-and-a-half weeks later, on October 29, he formally dissolved the Court of Oyer and Terminer. The court had heard thirty-one cases—only six against men—and had delivered death sentences against all the defendants.

Of the eleven still awaiting execution, five earned reprieves for confessing their guilt, two died in jail, two gained stays of execution because of pregnancy and were later reprieved, and one escaped. The last one, Tituba, was held in jail—as was related earlier—and later sold as a slave to pay for jail costs.

The Witch-Hunts End

On January 3, 1693, a newly formed Superior Court conducted additional trials in Salem Town. The new court convicted three more people of witchery, but Governor Sir William Phipps reprieved them (along with five other condemned witches as already noted).

In May, Sir William ordered the release of all accused witches still in prison, upon payment of jail fees, thereby ending the infamous Salem witch-hunt of 1692–93.

Afterword

Humble in the Dust

O N JANUARY 16, 1697, the provincial lieutenant governor, council, and assembly of Massachusetts Bay Colony declared a day of public fasting. They felt that God viewed their persecution of witches with displeasure, because he was "diminishing our substance, cutting short our harvest, blasting our most promising undertakings . . . and by his more immediate hand snatching away many out of our embraces by sudden and violent deaths." On the day of the fast, the twelve participating jurors signed a petition admitting taking the lives of those convicted on the basis of insufficient evidence. In hindsight's clear light, they had come to understand that the witch-hunt hysteria had deluded their judgment and that they had unfairly condemned the accused witches who had stood before them. The petition expressed their sorrow for taking up with "such evidence against the accused, as on further consideration, and better information, we justly fear was insufficient for touching the lives of any," thereby bringing upon themselves and "this People of the Lord, the guilt of innocent blood." It further stated:

> We do therefore hereby signify to all in general (and to the surviving sufferers in especial) our deep sense of, and sorrow for our errors, in acting on such evidence to the condemning of any person.

> And do hereby declare that we justly fear that we were sadly deluded and mistaken, for which we are much disquieted and distressed in our minds; and do therefore humbly beg forgiveness. . . .

We do heartily ask forgiveness of you all, whom we have justly offended, and do declare according to our present minds, we would none of us do such things again on such grounds for the whole world, praying you to accept this in satisfaction for our offense; and that you would bless the inheritance of the Lord, that He may be entreated for the land.

A conscience-stricken Judge Samuel Sewell joined the jurors in confessing his wrongdoing.

A Single Repentant Judge

While the judge stood to acknowledge his guilt, the minister of Boston's old South Church read Sewell's statement:

Samuel Sewell . . . being sensible as to the guilt contracted on the opening of the late commission of Oyer and Terminer at Salem (to which the order of this day relates) he is upon many accounts, more concerned than any he knows of, Desires to take the Blame and Shame of it, asking pardon of men, and especially desiring prayers that God, who has unlimited authority, would pardon that sin and all his other sins, personal and relative.

Sewell's confession distinguished him as the only participating judge in the Salem witch trials to offer public repentance.

Ann Putnam's Confession

As for the rest of those most instrumental in the conviction and execution of twenty adjudged witches, only Ann Putnam Jr., the dominant afflicted girl, came forward to seek forgiveness—and not until thirteen years later at the age of twenty-six.

In August 1706, seven years after the death of both Thomas and Ann Sr., the Reverend Joseph Green read young Ann's confession to the congregation in Salem Village church:

I desire to be humbled before God for that sad and humbling providence that befell my father's family in the year about 1692; that I then being in my childhood, should by such a providence of God, be made an instrument for the accusing of several persons of a grievous crime, whereby their lives were taken away from them, whom now I have just grounds and good reasons to believe they were innocent persons . . . but what I did was ignorantly, being deluded of satan. And particularly as I was a chief instrument of accusing of goodwife Nurse and her two sisters, I desire to lie in the dust, and to be humbled for it, in that I was the cause, with others, of so sad a calamity to them and their families; for which cause I desire to lie in the dust, and earnestly beg forgiveness of God, and from all those unto whom I have given just cause of sorrow and offense, whose relations were taken away or accused.

Ann Putnam Jr. suffered from chronic ill health and died eleven years later at the age of thirty-seven.

Four Reasons Why

For the nineteen people hanged and the one poor soul pressed to death, there are perhaps as many reasons now given for the causes of Salem's reign of diabolic horrors. Four reasons stand out as the most plausible explanations for the seeming madness.

One socioeconomic theory holds that the tragedy grew out of the repressed anger of low-subsistence farmers and tradesmen of Salem Village for the wealthier merchant class and gentry of Salem Town. A second explanation blames the climate of insecurities and uncertainties that prevailed while this isolated Puritan community changed rapidly into a commercial center. Psychologists and others offer a third hypothesis, focusing on the mental condition of the adolescent girls, comparing their antics and afflictions with paranormal events such as poltergeist phenomena thought to be often activated by teenage girls. Lastly, playwright Arthur Miller, in his play *The Crucible*—wherein he draws an analogy between the Salem witch trials and the McCarthy hearings of the 1950s—suggests that episodes of collective paranoia simply occur periodically, seemingly without reason or explanation.

Judge Samuel Sewell delivered a public apology for his part in the Salem witch trials.

"We Walked in Clouds"

The tragic affair at Salem Village, now more than three centuries old, ranks only as a speck on the larger blemish of humankind's long history of inhumanity toward its own. Yet, dwarfed as it may be by the greater tragedies of the Holocaust, the Inquisition, and even the mass suicide at Jonestown, the Salem witch affair still stirs the consciences of Americans today. And for generations to

THE WAGES OF WITCHCRAFT

Persons Hanged for Witchcraft in Salem Town in 1692

Bridget Bishop	June 10
Sarah Good	July 19
Elizabeth Howe	July 19
Susannah Martin	July 19
Rebecca Nurse	July 19
Sarah Wildes	July 19
George Burroughs	August 19
Martha Carrier	August 19
George Jacobs Sr.	August 19
John Proctor	August 19
John Willard	August 19
Giles Corey	September 19 (pressed to death)
Martha Corey	September 22
Mary Easty	September 22
Alice Parker	September 22
Mary Parker	September 22
Ann Pudeator	September 22
Margaret Scott	September 22
Wilmot Redd	September 22
Samuel Wardwell	September 22

Persons Accused of Witchcraft Who Died in Jail

Sarah Osborne	May 10, 1692
Roger Toothaker	June 16, 1692
Ann Foster	December 3, 1692
Linda Dustin	March 10, 1693

Sarah Good's unnamed infant died prior to July 19, 1692.

come, Americans will likely still question how the good people of Salem Village could have fostered such acts of evil.

Perhaps the Reverend John Hale of Beverly said it best in 1697, when he wrote, "We walked in clouds and could not see our way. And we have most cause to be humbled for error . . . which cannot be retrieved."

Glossary

apparition: A ghostly figure; a specter.

familiar: A spirit slave, sometimes embodied in human shape, sometimes appearing as a cat, dog, raven, or other animal; a familiar spirit.

Goodman: An archaic term for the master of a household.

Goodwife: An archaic term for the mistress of a household; often shortened to Goody or Gammer.

hysteria: Unmanageable fear or emotional excess.

image magic: The use of a person's own body instead of a doll (as in the practice of voodoo) to inflict harm on others, by pinching, biting, sticking pins, and so on.

magic: The use of means—such as charms or spells—believed to have supernatural power over natural forces; see also *sorcery* and *witchcraft*.

ordinary: An archaic term for an inn, restaurant, or tavern.

oyer and terminer: A French phrase meaning "to hear and determine," as in Court of Oyer and Terminer.

sabbat: A midnight gathering of witches or sorcerers held especially in medieval and Renaissance times to renew allegiance to the devil through mystic rites and orgies.

sorcery: The use of power gained through the assistance or control of evil spirits; see also *magic* and *witchcraft*.

specter: A visible disembodied spirit; an apparition.

spectral evidence: Evidence based solely on claims of evil acts committed by a person's specter.

witchcraft: The practice of sorcery or magic; see also *magic* and *sorcery*.

witch's book: A book signed by witches to enlist in the service of the devil.

witch's cake: A cake of meal and urine used as a test to detect the presence of witches, familiars, or other agents of the devil.

Timeline

1691

November: Tituba's circle forms and storytelling sessions start at the Reverend Samuel Parris's parsonage in Salem Village.

1692

January: The girls of Tituba's circle begin to act strangely; the Parrises call several doctors to the parsonage to diagnose the girls' afflictions.

February 25: Mary Sibley asks John and Tituba Indian to prepare a witch's cake to learn what is afflicting the local girls; shortly thereafter, the girls name three women as their tormentors.

March 1: Preliminary examinations on witch charges held for Sarah Good, Sarah Osborne, and Tituba; Good and Osborne deny charges; Tituba confesses to being a witch.

March 21: Martha Corey brought to preliminary hearing and denies charges; she attempts to be tricky but is caught in a lie.

March 24: Rebecca Nurse arrested and brought to hearing; she maintains her innocence and is held for trial; four-year-old Dorcas Good accused of witchcraft, arrested, and imprisoned.

April 11: Sarah Cloyce and Elizabeth Proctor appear for preliminary hearing and claim innocence; the afflicted girls cry out on Elizabeth's husband John; Cloyce and both Proctors sent to prison to await trial.

May 10: George Jacobs Sr. brought before magistrates on witch charges made by Sarah Churchill, his seventeen-year-old servant girl.

May 29: Elizabeth Howe arrested and charged with tormenting Ann Putnam Jr., Mercy Lewis, and Mary Walcott.

June 2: Governor Sir William Phipps appoints a special Court of Oyer and Terminer to try the accused witches; Bridget Bishop becomes the first person to be tried on witch charges.

June 10: Bridget Bishop is hanged on Gallows Hill, the first of nineteen accused witches to be so executed.

June 30: Sarah Good, Rebecca Nurse, Susannah Martin, Elizabeth Howe, and Sarah Wildes face the court as witch trials resume.

July 19: Sarah Good, Rebecca Nurse, Susannah Martin, Elizabeth Howe, and Sarah Wildes are hanged on Gallows Hill.

August 5: George Burroughs, John and Elizabeth Proctor, George Jacobs Sr., John Willard, and Martha Carrier are tried as witches, found guilty, and sentenced to hang.

August 19: George Burroughs, John Proctor, George Jacobs Sr., John Willard, and Martha Carrier are hanged on Gallows Hill; Elizabeth Proctor is spared because of her pregnancy.

September 9: Martha Corey, Mary Easty, Alice Parker, Ann Pudeator, Dorcas Hoar, and Mary Bradbury are tried as witches, found guilty, and sentenced to hang.

September 17: The court delivers death sentences on Margaret Scott, Wilmot Redd, Samuel Wardwell, Mary Parker, Abigail Falkner, Rebecca Eames, Mary Lacy, Ann Foster, and Abigail Hobbes; Giles Corey refuses to enter a plea.

September 19: Giles Corey pressed to death by stones piled on him for refusing to enter a plea.

September 22: Martha Corey, Mary Easty, Alice Parker, Mary Parker, Ann Pudeator, Margaret Scott, Wilmot Redd, and Samuel Wardwell are hanged. These are the last hangings in Salem Town.

October 12: Governor Sir William Phipps orders a moratorium on all witch trials.

October 29: Governor Phipps formally dissolves the Court of Oyer and Terminer.

For Further Reading

Richard Daley, ed., *Tales of Witchcraft*. London: Michael O'Mara Books Limited, 1991. Reprint, Edison, NJ: Castle Books, 1994. A collection of macabre and frightening stories by such masters of the supernatural genre as Stephen King, Robert Bloch, M. R. James, Saki, E. F. Benson, and others. These chilling stories leave open to question "more things in heaven and earth than are dreamt of in our normal, everyday philosophies."

Arthur Miller, *The Crucible*, in *Arthur Miller*. New York: Quality Paperback Book Club, 1995. The distinguished American playwright "explores the threshold between individual guilt and mass hysteria, comparing the Salem witch trials of the seventeenth century to the McCarthy hearings that were making headlines as [he] was writing the play" in 1953.

Montague Summers, *The History of Witchcraft*. University Books, 1956. Reprint, New York: Citadel Press, 1993. The Reverend Montague Summers, a Roman Catholic priest, presents views on witchcraft and demonology far different from Catholic sourcebooks and present-day representatives of the church. Dr. Summers writes from a perspective described by critics as "a medieval viewpoint, an absolute and complete belief in witchcraft and, hence, in the supernatural." Subjects covered in this classic work include: the Witch, Heretic and Anarchist; Demons and Familiars; the Sabbat; the Witch in Holy Writ; Diabolic Possession and Modern Spiritism; and the Witch in Dramatic Literature.

———, *Witchcraft and Black Magic*. London: Rider & Company, Reprint, London: Senate, 1995. The author's coverage of occult and supernatural topics spans a wide range and includes such arcane subjects as pacts with the devil, sacrilege, blood, the evil eye, the Black Mass, and wax images.

Works Consulted

Leonard R. N. Ashley, *The Complete Book of Magic and Witchcraft.* New York: Barricade Books, 1986. Professor Ashley presents the world of mysterious forces, strange beliefs, and superstitions as old as time and as new as a Stephen King fantasy.

Paul Boyer and Stephen Nissenbaum, eds., *Salem Village Witchcraft.* Belmont, CA: Wadsworth, 1972. Reprint, Boston: Northeastern University Press, 1993. The editors present a scholarly collection of transcripts of the preliminary proceedings and much of the testimony against five accused witches.

John Putnam Demos, *Entertaining Satan: Witchcraft and the Culture of Early New England.* New York: Oxford University Press, 1982. Demos analyzes over a hundred cases of witchcraft in seventeenth-century New England in an attempt to understand the kind of society and the kind of culture in which witchcraft had a place.

Chadwick Hansen, *Witchcraft at Salem.* New York: George Braziller, 1969. Hansen provides an innovative and thoughtful look at that turbulent episode in the history of Massachusetts.

Frances Hill, *A Delusion of Satan: The Full Story of the Salem Witch Trials.* New York: Doubleday, 1995. A compelling account of the witch-hunt and trials that terrorized and tormented the Puritans of Salem Village in the horrifying period between 1691 and 1693.

Carol F. Karlsen, *The Devil in the Shape of a Woman: Witchcraft in Colonial New England.* New York: W. W. Norton & Company, 1987. Reprint, New York: Vintage Books, 1989. Professor Carol Karlsen of the University of Michigan draws a rich portrait of the women prosecuted as witches in the late seventeenth century.

Richard Marshall, *Witchcraft: The History and Mythology.* New York: Crescent Books, 1995. An exploration of the witch's universe, from classical Greek legend to present-day practitioners of Wicca; lavishly illustrated.

Frank McLynn, *Famous Trials: Cases That Made History*. Pleas-antville, NY: The Reader's Digest Association, 1995. This fascinating volume offers vivid re-creations of thirty-four famous trials spanning two thousand years.

Fred Pelka, "The 'Women's Holocaust,'" *Humanist*, September/October 1992, pp. 5–9, 32. This lengthy article purports and supports the premise that witch-hunting is primarily a history of the oppression of women.

"The Salem Witch-Trials: Misogyny, Ergot or Envy?" *Economist* 16, May 1992, p. 31. This article briefly examines recent claims as to the causes of witchcraft at Salem.

Hans Sebald, *Witch-Children: From Salem Witch-Hunts to Modern Courtrooms*. Amherst, NY: Prometheus Books, 1995. Sebald explores the phenomenon of children "in a position to wreak havoc on the lives of innocent persons."

Marion L. Starkey, *The Devil in Massachusetts: A Modern Enquiry into the Salem Witch Trials*. New York: Alfred A. Knopf, 1949. Reprint, New York: Anchor Books, 1989. Starkey, an author, editor, and educator, applies modern psychiatric knowledge and an unerring sense of drama to create an engaging and authentic historical narrative.

John M. Taylor, *The Witchcraft Delusion: The Story of the Witchcraft Persecutions in Seventeenth-Century New England, Including Original Trial Transcripts*. New York: Gramercy Books, 1995. Using actual trial records and original testimony, Taylor "expertly re-creates this bizarre period in American history."

Selma R. Williams and Pamela Williams Adelman, *Riding the Nightmare: Women & Witchcraft from the Old World to Colonial Salem*. New York: Atheneum, 1978. Reprint, New York: Harper Perennial, 1992. The authors present an intriguing overview of "how myths, folk art, popular tracts, church dogma, and politics linked up during the decline of agrarian society to brew a craze that sent as many as a million people—90 percent of them women—to the gallows."

Index

Picture Credits

About the Author

Earle Rice Jr. attended San Jose City College and Foothill College on the San Francisco peninsula, after serving nine years with the U.S. Marine Corps.

He has authored nineteen books for young adults, including fast-action fiction and adaptations of *Dracula*, *All Quiet on the Western Front*, and *The Grapes of Wrath*. Mr. Rice has written several books for Lucent, including *The Cuban Revolution* and seven books in the popular *Great Battles* series. He has also written articles and short stories and has previously worked for several years as a technical writer.

Mr. Rice is a former senior design engineer in the aerospace industry who now devotes full time to his writing. He lives in Julian, California, with his wife, daughter, two granddaughters, five cats, and a dog.